W9-CLX-788

**COURSE 2**

*MOVING MATH FORWARD THROUGH CRITICAL THINKING AND EXPLORATION*

# Puzzling Proportions

## Focusing on Rates, Percents and Similarity

Suzanne H. Chapin

M. Katherine Gavin

Linda Jensen Sheffield

Kendall Hunt
publishing company

## ACKNOWLEDGMENTS

## Math Innovations Writing Team

### Authors

Suzanne H. Chapin

M. Katherine Gavin

Linda Jensen Sheffield

### Project Manager

Janice M. Vuolo

### Teacher Edition Team

Jacob J. Whitmore

Ann Marie Spinelli

Alice J. Gabbard

### Writing Assistants

Kathy Dorkin

Jane Paulin

### Mathematics Editor

Kathleen G. Snook

### Assessment Specialist

Nancy Anderson

### Advisory Board

Jerry P. Becker

Janet Beissinger

Diane J. Briars

Ann Lawrence

Ira J. Papick

## Kendall Hunt

publishing company

www.kendallhunt.com

Send all inquiries to:

4050 Westmark Drive

Dubuque, IA 52004-1840

1-800-542-6657

Copyright © 2010 by Kendall Hunt Publishing Company

ISBN 978-0-7575-6704-9

Production Date: 8/2017
Printed by LSI.
United States of America
Batch number: 426704

# Puzzling Proportions:
## Focusing on Rates, Percents and Similarity
# Table of Contents

# UNIT GOALS

**STUDENT** EDITION

## Puzzling Proportions: Focusing on Rates, Percents and Similarity

### After studying this unit, you should be able to:

- Compare two quantities using diagrams, ratios and rates.
- Find the fixed number value of a ratio.
- Solve ratio problems using proportions, equations and equivalent ratios.
- Calculate rates and unit rates.
- Represent proportional relationships using tables, graphs and equations.
  - Understand and make scale drawings.
  - Understand the characteristics of similar figures and how to find values for missing dimensions in these figures.

- Graph a proportional relationship and understand that the slope of the resulting line is the constant of proportionality.
- Interpret and classify direct variation relationships.
- Use percents that are less than 1% and greater than 100% to solve problems.
- Solve percent problems.
- Understand sales, markups, markdowns and percent increase and decrease.

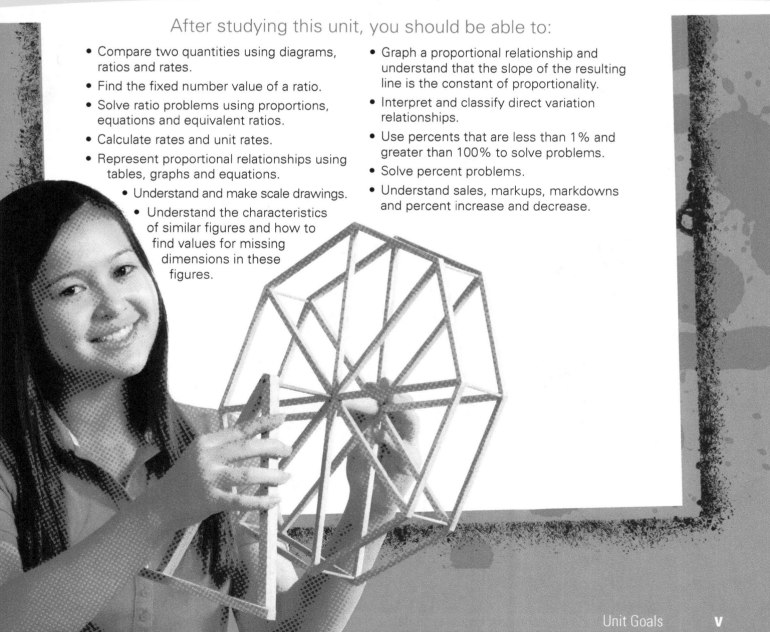

# Dear Student Mathematician,

You use ratios and rates all the time. You use them to calculate the sale price of a new bicycle or a tip at a restaurant.

Proportions relate two ratios. You can use proportions to find the dimensions of a model car that is based on a real car. When you use proportions, you often use ideas from multiplication, division, fractions, measurement and algebra.

In this unit, *Puzzling Proportions: Focusing on Rates, Percents and Similarity*, you will explore relationships among part-to-part and part-to-whole ratios. You will learn about similar figures, and how to draw figures to scale and read a floor plan. You will investigate percents, equivalent fractions and proportions. Finally, you will extend your knowledge of graphing as you learn about direct variation and slope.

We hope you enjoy learning about rates, percents and similarity, and how these ideas are applied in a range of situations.

Mathematically yours,
The Authors

*Suzanne H. Chapin*

*M. Katherine Gavin*

*Linda Sheffield*

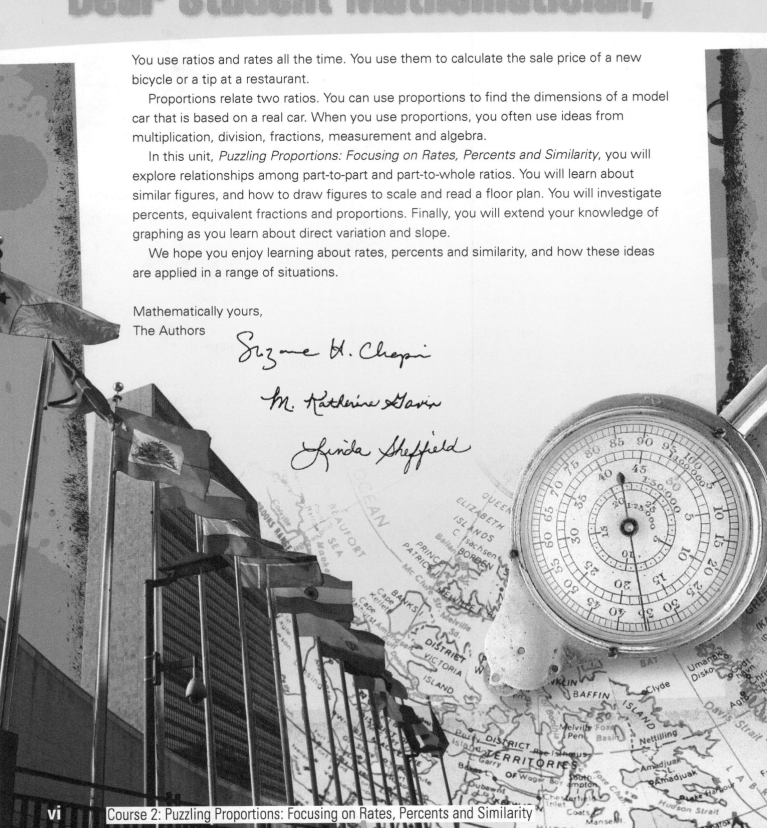

# Comparing Quantities

Almost every day we compare quantities. Is this video game a better buy? Which store has the best price for DVDs? How many batches of cookies do I need if one batch makes two dozen cookies?

In this section you will learn how to compare two numbers. These comparisons can be expressed as fractions, decimals, percents and as ratios and rates.

## LESSON 1.1 Ratios

 **Start It Off**

1. **a)** Write a ratio that compares the number of brown eggs to the number of white eggs.

   **b)** The ratio you wrote is called a part-to-part ratio. What are the parts that are being compared?

2. **a)** Write a ratio that compares the number of white eggs to the total number of eggs.

   **b)** The ratio you wrote is called a part-to-whole ratio. What is the part and what is the whole that are being compared?

3. Write another part-to-part ratio and another part-to-whole ratio about the eggs.

4. Define the term *ratio*.

**MATHEMATICALLY SPEAKING**
- ▶ part-to-part ratio
- ▶ part-to-whole ratio
- ▶ ratio

 **Let's Review**

There are several ways to express a ratio:

3 to 4        3 : 4        $\frac{3}{4}$

Fraction notation is usually used for a part-to-whole comparison. The colon notation often indicates a part-to-part comparison. Any of the notations can be used for any type of ratio, so you should use the context of a problem to determine the type of comparison that is being made.

In earlier grades, did you use pattern blocks to represent fractions? Pattern blocks can also be used to illustrate ratios. Below is a design made from one trapezoid and three green triangles that looks a bit like mountains.

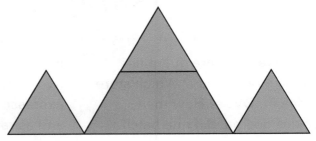

The ratio of number of trapezoids to number of green triangles in the mountain picture is 1:3. We can also say that the ratio of number of triangles to number of trapezoids is 3:1. These are part-to-part ratios since they compare parts of the set.

The ratio of number of trapezoids to total number of blocks in the picture is 1:4. The ratio of green triangles to blocks is 3:4. These are part-to-whole ratios since they compare a part to the total number of blocks. You can switch the order of the comparison and compare the total number of blocks to the number of trapezoids (4:1) or the total number of blocks to the number of green triangles (4:3).

In a ratio, it is important to know what is being compared and in what order.

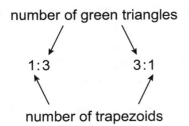

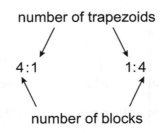

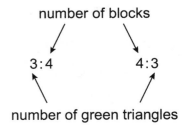

You can use copies of the mountain design to make new designs. Examine the picture below.

1. **a)** Use more blocks to create your own design using the mountain design.

   **b)** How many copies of the original design did you use?

   **c)** How many trapezoids did you use? How many green triangles? How many blocks?

   **d)** How are the number of copies of the original mountain design and the total number of blocks related?

2. Copy and complete this table.

**DESIGN DATA**

| Copies of the Original Mountain Design | Number of Trapezoids | Number of Green Triangles | Total Number of Blocks | Ratio of Trapezoids to Triangles |
|---|---|---|---|---|
| 1 | 1 | 3 | 4 | 1:3 |
| 2 | 2 | 6 | 8 | 2:6 |
| 3 | | | | |
| 4 | | | 16 | |
| 5 | | | | |

   **a)** Describe the numerical patterns that occur in each column.

   **b)** How are the numbers in each row related?

3. **a)** Copy and complete the extension of the Design Data table below.

**DESIGN DATA**

| Copies of the Original Mountain Design | Number of Trapezoids | Number of Green Triangles | Total Number of Blocks | Ratio of Trapezoids to Triangles |
|---|---|---|---|---|
|  | 9 |  |  |  |
|  |  | 39 |  |  |
|  |  |  | 60 |  |
|  |  | 108 |  |  |
|  | 152 |  |  |  |
|  |  |  |  | 16 : 48 |
| n |  |  |  |  |

**b)** Explain the patterns you noted for *n* copies of the original design.

Generic diagrams can be used to represent the relationships in a ratio. This is especially useful when a ratio compares things that aren't easy to draw such as the number of jazz songs to number of soul songs on an album. It is important to label the parts.

Example

Use bar diagrams to represent ratios.

The diagram shows the 1 : 3 ratio, as in the mountain design. Each square in the diagram represents one pattern block.

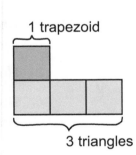

1 trapezoid

3 triangles

Each square in the bar diagram can also represent more than one block. The bar diagrams below still show the ratio of 1 to 3.

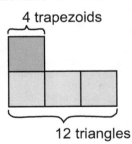

4 trapezoids

12 triangles

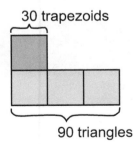

30 trapezoids

90 triangles

If each square represents 4 pattern blocks, the bar diagram on the left shows the ratio 4 : 12.
If each square represents 30 pattern blocks, the bar diagram on the right shows the ratio 30 : 90.
In both cases the basic relationship between trapezoids and triangles remains 1 : 3.

**4. a)** How many copies of the mountain design are needed to make a 4:12 ratio of trapezoids to green triangles?

**b)** How many copies are needed to make the 30:90 ratio?

**5. a)** To keep the 1:3 ratio of trapezoids to green triangles, how many blocks does each square below represent?

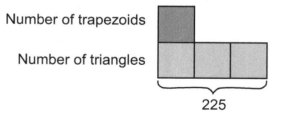

Number of trapezoids

Number of triangles

225

**b)** How many pattern blocks would you need to make the design represented by this bar diagram?

**6. a)** A block design uses a total of 48 pattern blocks and keeps the same 1:3 ratio. How many blocks are green triangles?

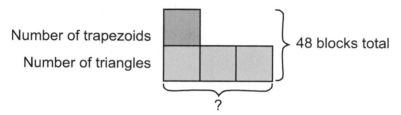

Number of trapezoids

Number of triangles

48 blocks total

?

**b)** Explain your answer to Part a.

**7. a)** The total number of blocks used to make a design using the 1:3 ratio is 92. How many trapezoids and green triangles are needed?

**b)** Describe your strategy for solving Part a.

**8.** Make up another problem similar to Question 7. Choose a ratio of trapezoids to triangles and give the total number of blocks. The number of blocks should be greater than 100. Solve your problem.

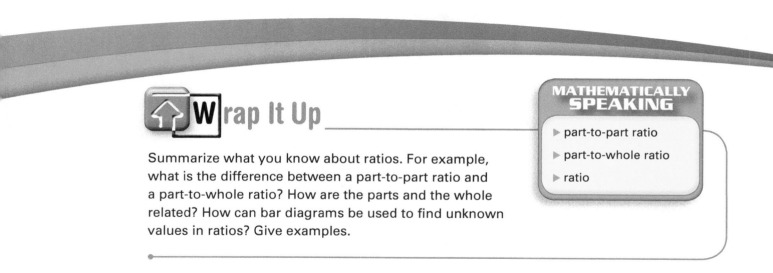

# Wrap It Up

Summarize what you know about ratios. For example, what is the difference between a part-to-part ratio and a part-to-whole ratio? How are the parts and the whole related? How can bar diagrams be used to find unknown values in ratios? Give examples.

**MATHEMATICALLY SPEAKING**

▶ part-to-part ratio

▶ part-to-whole ratio

▶ ratio

**Write About It**

1. Kong built a design using triangles and squares in a ratio of 2 : 3. He used a total of 60 blocks in his design. How many triangles and squares did Kong use? Explain your solution method.

2. Most United Nations flags have a length-to-width ratio of 3 : 2. Draw and label a bar diagram to show this relationship. List the dimensions of two flags that have this length-to-width ratio that might be displayed outside the United Nations.

3. Write two ratios that compare the number of notebooks to the number of books in your backpack. Label the ratios.

4. Why is the order of the numbers in a ratio so important?

5. The ratio of boys to girls in a middle school soccer program is 8 : 7. If there are 135 students in the program, how many of them are girls?

6. Determine the missing values in each ratio.

a)

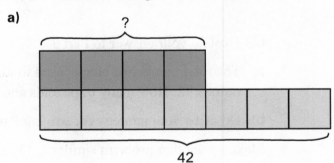

42

b)

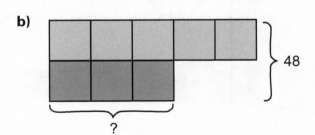

48

?

c)

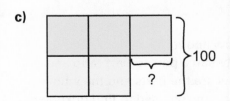

100

?

7. Two cousins earned $1,800 mowing lawns one summer. Based on the amount of work they each did, they decide to share the money based on a ratio of 2 : 3. How much money should each cousin get? Draw a bar diagram to help you.

8. **a)** The weight of Package A is $\frac{3}{5}$ the weight of Package B. If the two packages together weigh 120 pounds, how much does Package A weigh?

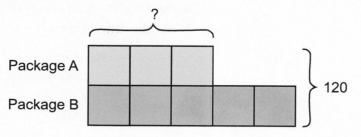

   **b)** Explain how to use the bar diagram to solve the problem.

9. Identify if each ratio is a part-to-part or part-to-whole ratio.

   **a)** In the Pacific states, the ratio of bicycle commuters to all commuters is 1 : 100.

   **b)** A gear ratio on a bicycle is the number of teeth on the front chain ring to the number of teeth on the rear chain ring.

   **c)** A bicycle odometer (which records distance traveled) has a ratio of 1,690 : 1. The ratio represents the number of times a wheel turns per mile.

   **d)** The ratio of the height of a person to the height of her bicycle is 3 : 2.

   **e)** 85 out of every 100 children wear a bicycle helmet when riding.

10. Ms. Zito, a seventh grade math teacher, has a jar containing erasers and pencils on her desk. The jar is pictured at the right.

a) What is the ratio of erasers to pencils in the jar?

b) Compare the number of erasers to the number of items in the jar. Write the ratio as a fraction.

c) Suppose you have another jar with the same ratio of erasers to pencils, but it contains 272 items. How many pencils are in the jar?

11. a) Write two different part-to-part ratios about the boys and girls in the picture.

b) Describe the picture using two part-to-whole ratios. For each ratio, indicate what is being compared.

Think Beyond

12. Winston, Lad and Toby have MP3 players. The ratio of the number of songs they have is $4:5:6$ (Winston to Lad to Toby). Toby has 60 more songs than Winston. Find the total number of songs they have.

13. What is the difference between ft.² and ft.³? When are each of these labels used?

14. A pool with dimensions of 24' by 8' by 10' is being filled with water. When it is filled halfway, the filters are turned on. How much water is in the pool when the filters are turned on?

    **A.** 480 ft.³

    **B.** 960 ft.³

    **C.** 240 ft.³

    **D.** 1,920 ft.³

15. Estimate the sum, then find the exact sum: $-1\frac{2}{5} + (-3\frac{17}{20})$. Show your work.

16. Place each set of decimals in order from least to greatest.

    **a)** $0.\overline{61}$; $0.61$; $0.6\overline{1}$; $0.611$; $0.6161$

    **b)** $-0.93$, $-0.9\overline{3}$, $-0.\overline{93}$, $-0.\overline{9}$

17. Simplify the expression $-6(\frac{1}{3}h - 2)$ using the distributive property.

# Multiplicative Comparisons

## Start It Off

Two children were born on the same day. Katie was 20 inches long and weighed 8 pounds at birth. Alfred was 18 inches long and weighed 7 pounds at birth.

At their 6-month checkup, Katie is 26 inches long and weighs 16 pounds. Alfred is 24 inches long and weighs 14 pounds.

1. Which child increased most in length? Which child gained the most weight?

2. Who grew the most during this 6-month period? Explain.

## Comparisons with Ratios

There are many ways to compare numbers. For example, finding how many more soccer players there are than basketball players involves subtracting one number from another.

Another way to compare two numbers is to use multiplication. For example, at 6 months both Alfred and Katie weigh 2 *times* as much as they did at birth. Baby Alfred is $\frac{4}{3}$ *times* as long as he was at birth. These are known as multiplicative comparisons.

You can compare the two numbers in a ratio using multiplication. For example, you state that the value of one quantity in a ratio is "so many times" the value of the other quantity. This multiplicative comparison is sometimes referred to as the value of a ratio. To find the value of a ratio, divide the first number by the second number.

Example 1

A pound cake recipe calls for 5 cups of flour for every 2 cups of sugar. The ratio of number of cups of flour to number of cups of sugar is 5 : 2. The number of cups of sugar is the base for comparison purposes.

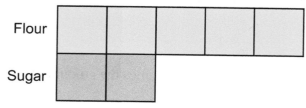

The bar diagram compares 5 to 2. To find the value of the ratio, divide 5 by 2.

$5 \div 2 = \frac{5}{2}$ or $2\frac{1}{2}$ or 2.5

The value of this ratio tells you there are 2.5 times as many cups of flour as cups of sugar.

Example 2

You can change the order of the numbers in a ratio and change the base used. The number of cups of sugar is how many times the number of cups of flour?

The ratio of cups of sugar to cups of flour is 2 : 5. To find the value of the ratio, divide 2 by 5.

$2 \div 5 = \frac{2}{5}$ or 0.4

There are $\frac{2}{5}$ times as many cups of sugar as cups of flour. The amount of sugar is $\frac{2}{5}$ or 40% the amount of flour. The value of 2 : 5 is different from the value of 5 : 2.

1. What is meant by the value of a ratio? Why are there two different values in Examples 1 and 2?

For each of the ratios in Questions 2–5, first draw and label a bar diagram. Then answer the questions.

2. To make salad dressing, you combine oil and vinegar in a ratio of 3 : 1.

   a) Which ingredient do you use more of?

   b) The amount of oil used is how many times the amount of vinegar used?

   c) The amount of vinegar used is how many times the amount of oil used?

   d) If you use 1 cup of oil to make a batch of dressing, what fraction of a cup of vinegar will you need?

3. The ratio of boys to girls on the debating team is 4 : 5.

   a) What is the value of the boy-to-girl ratio?

   b) Write a sentence that describes the number of boys as a multiple of the number of girls.

   c) Write a sentence that describes the number of boys as a percent of the number of girls.

   d) Write a sentence that multiplicatively compares the number of girls to the number of boys.

4. Alison and Richard are cousins. Alison's weight is $\frac{3}{8}$ of Richard's weight.

   a) What does the statement, "Alison's weight is $\frac{3}{8}$ of Richard's weight" mean?

   b) What is the ratio of Alison's weight to Richard's weight?

   c) What is the ratio of Richard's weight to Alison's weight?

   d) Write an equation that compares Richard's weight to Alison's weight.

   e) Give possible weights for both Alison and Richard.

**5.** Ming and John both have stamp collections. Ming has $1\frac{1}{2}$ times the number of stamps John has. What ratio represents the number of John's stamps compared to the number of Ming's stamps?

**6.** Single numbers can be used to show the relationship between two amounts in a ratio. Using one of the questions in this lesson, explain how the order of a ratio affects its value.

# Equivalent Ratios

Equivalent ratios show the same relationship between two comparisons. Equivalent ratios have the same ratio value. You can form equivalent ratios for part-to-part and part-to-whole ratios.

You can form equivalent ratios by multiplying or dividing both numbers in one ratio by the same value. You can divide both numbers in a ratio by a common factor to form a simplified ratio. A simplified ratio is just like a simplified fraction; it is in the most reduced form. You can make sense of equivalent ratios using bar diagrams, tables and symbols.

---

**Example 1**

Find a ratio equivalent to $2:6$.

• Divide both numbers in this ratio by the common factor of 2.

• The ratios $2:6$ and $1:3$ are equivalent because they simplify to the ratio value $\frac{1}{3}$. Both ratios show the same multiplicative comparison.

• Bar diagrams can be used to show that both ratios show the same multiplicative relationship. The ratio 2 to 6 is made up of two copies of the simplified ratio $1:3$.

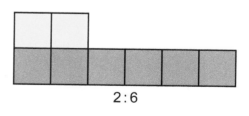
2:6

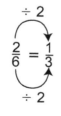
$\div 2$
$$\frac{2}{6} = \frac{1}{3}$$
$\div 2$

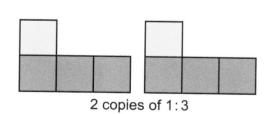
2 copies of 1:3

---

Example 2

Find other ratios equivalent to $2:6$.

To find equivalent ratios, multiply or divide both parts of the ratio by the same number.

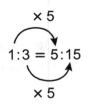

It may help to put the ratios into a table.

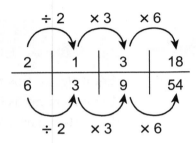

Some of the ratios equivalent to $2:6$ are $10:30 = 8:24 = 1:3 = 3:9 = 18:54$. What others can you find?

Solve the following problems by using what you have learned.

7. Leanne wants to "scale down" the following ratios. Find equivalent ratios of each ratio by dividing both parts of the ratio by the same number.

   a) $32:36$

   b) $14:21$

   c) $36:54$

   d) $24:27$

8. Give the value of each ratio as a decimal.

   a) $1:3$

   b) $5:15$

   c) $13:39$

   d) $24:72$

   e) $4.2:12.6$

   f) What do you notice? Why does this pattern happen?

**9. a)** Divide the second number by the first number in each of the ratios in Question 8. Record the quotients.

   **b)** Compare these numbers to your answers in Question 8. What do you notice? Explain your results.

**10.** Tom and Amy were competing to see who was the better free-throw shooter. Tom made 8 out of 10 shots and Amy made 15 out of 18 shots.

   **a)** Edward said that he could "scale up" a ratio by multiplying both parts of the ratio by the same number. Describe how you can "scale up" to find who is the better free-throw shooter.

   **b)** Scale down both ratios by reducing them to simplest form. Use these ratios to find the better free-throw shooter.

   **c)** Find the value of each of the ratios to settle on the best free-throw shooter.

   **d)** Which method do you prefer? Why?

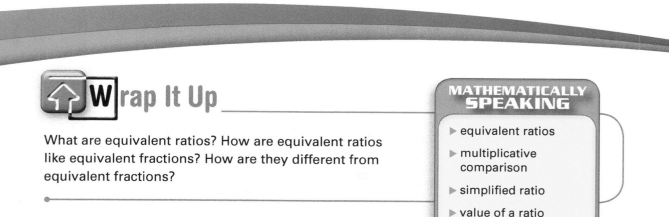

## Wrap It Up

What are equivalent ratios? How are equivalent ratios like equivalent fractions? How are they different from equivalent fractions?

**MATHEMATICALLY SPEAKING**

▶ equivalent ratios

▶ multiplicative comparison

▶ simplified ratio

▶ value of a ratio

 **Write About It**

1. The ratio $2:8$ compares the amount of nylon and fleece in a jacket. Sasha wonders why $2:8$, $\frac{1}{4}$ and 0.25 can all be used to compare these two quantities. Explain to Sasha using pictures, words and/or symbols how both a ratio and a number can compare these different amounts.

For Questions 2–4, a ratio comparing the amount of money Kevin has to the amount of money Alisha has is given. Answer the following questions for each ratio.

   **a)** Draw a bar diagram to compare the quantities multiplicatively.

   **b)** Write a sentence that describes the amount of money Kevin has as a fraction of the amount of money Alisha has.

2. $4:3$

3. $2:7$

4. $10:5$

5. How does comparing two numbers multiplicatively differ from finding their difference? Compare 12 and 4 as an example.

6. What is the ratio of the length of string C to the length of string D? Measure in centimeters.

    String C

    String D

7. There are 50% as many cats as dogs on a farm.

   **a)** Write two statements comparing the number of cats and dogs using fractions and decimals.

   **b)** What is the ratio of dogs to cats on the farm?

   **c)** Could there be 2 dogs and 4 cats on the farm? Why or why not?

8. Andrea is $\frac{4}{3}$ times as tall as Elise. Find the ratio of Elise's height to Andrea's height.

9. The ratio of black keys to white keys on a keyboard is 10:14. Write two comparison sentences about this ratio.

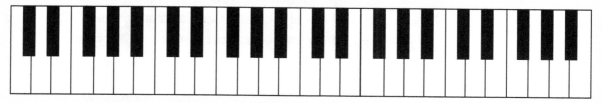

10. 78 students went on a field trip to a museum. 60 of them were girls.

   a) Find the ratio of boys to girls who went on the trip.

   b) Write a sentence that multiplicatively compares the number of boys to the number of girls. Use a decimal.

11. There are 5 times as many girls as boys in the school band.

   a) What is the ratio of the number of girls to the number of boys in the band?

   b) Write a sentence that expresses the number of boys as a fraction of the number of girls.

12. At the local zoo there are two snakes. Each year on July 1, they are given a checkup, and their lengths are measured. Samantha Snake was 4 feet long last July but is now 7 feet long. Sam Snake was 5 feet long but is now 8 feet long. Which snake grew the most during the past year? Explain.

13. In a taste test, 40 students preferred the sports drink Energize. 60 students preferred the sports drink Powerburst. Write a sentence comparing these students using:

   a) ratios

   b) fractions

   c) decimals

   d) percents

   e) differences

14. List four ratios that are equivalent to 36:24. Use multiplication to find two of the ratios and division to find the other two ratios.

15. Simplify these ratios.

   a) 32:24          c) 45:55

   b) 63:28          d) 48:64

16. Amy thinks that she is a better free-throw shooter than Candice. Amy made 14 out of 18 shots. Candice made 9 out of 12 shots. Based on these ratios, who is the better free-throw shooter?

17. All official U.S. flags have a length-to-width ratio of 19:10.

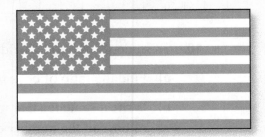

a) If the width of one official flag is 120 cm, find the length.

b) If the length of another official flag is 171 cm, find the width.

c) A store sells flags that are 38 inches by 20 inches and 57 cm by 30 cm. Are the ratios 38:20 and 57:30 equivalent to 19:10? Why or why not?

18. The largest U.S. flag is in Long Beach, California. It measures 505 ft. by 225 ft. and weighs 3,000 pounds! Is this an official U.S. flag? Explain.

 Think Beyond

19. Deacon and Kinne were comparing the money in their savings accounts. Deacon's amount of money is $\frac{3}{5}$ of Kinne's amount of money.

a) What is the ratio of Deacon's savings to Kinne's savings?

b) If Kinne gives $\frac{1}{2}$ of her money to Deacon, what will be the new ratio of Deacon's savings to Kinne's savings?

20. Find the answer using mental math techniques.

    **a)** $2.1 + 3.2 + 1.9 =$

    **b)** $6.7 - 2.0 - 1.4 - 1.3 =$

    **c)** $8.2 - 1.8 - 2.0 + 3.8 - 2.2 =$

    **d)** $1.5 + 2.5 - 4 + 6.5 - 2.5 - 1.5 =$

21. An apple pie in the shape of a circle fits perfectly within a square box that is $11\frac{3}{4}$ inches on every side. What is the radius of the pie? What is the area of the top of the pie?

22. Write each fraction as a decimal and percent.

    **a)** $\frac{2}{5}$

    **b)** $\frac{5}{15}$

    **c)** $\frac{3}{25}$

23. Which of these values is closest to 0?

    **A.** $\frac{2}{11}$

    **B.** $-0.18$

    **C.** $0.105$

    **D.** $-\frac{1}{8}$

24. **a)** Make a table of data that relates the stage number ($n$) to the number of line segments ($s$) in the pattern. This pattern continues by adding this shape  to each subsequent stage.

    Stage 0        Stage 1                Stage 2                        Stage 3

    **b)** Write an equation that links the number of line segments to the stage number.

## Start It Off

1. Which is the better buy for a sports drink? Explain.

$2.70
18 oz.

$3.00
20 oz.

"The Gatorade is his."

© CartoonStock Ltd, www.cartoonstock.com

2. Determine the best buy in a different way. Show your work.

## Exploring Rates

How fast can you trace? To test your manual dexterity rate, see how many stars, like the ones below, you can trace in 20 seconds. Stars must be traced accurately by going over the lines. A star is made up of ten line segments, so each segment is 0.1 of a star. Partial stars may be included in your count, but count only tenths that are completely covered.

1. **a)** Estimate the number of stars you think you can trace in 20 seconds.

   **b)** Work with a partner. One of you should trace, while the other keeps track of the time. Then, switch roles.

**MATHEMATICALLY SPEAKING**

▶ **rate**

▶ **unit rate**

**Let's Review**

A rate is a type of ratio that uses different types of measures. For example, $3.50 for 2 bags of flour is a rate that compares dollars to bags. A unit rate is a comparison to the number 1. To make this rate a unit rate, divide both numbers by 2.

The unit rate of $1.75 to 1 bag means that it costs $1.75 for 1 bag of flour. You can find a unit rate by scaling a ratio up or down so that second part of the ratio is 1. You can also find a unit rate by dividing the first number in the rate by the second number. The value of the rate is equivalent to the unit rate, 1.75.

÷ 2

| Dollars | 3.50 | 1.75 |
|---|---|---|
| Number of bags | 2 | 1 |

÷ 2

**2. a)** How many stars did you trace? Make sure to include the tenths of the stars that you drew. Write that number of stars over 20 seconds. This is the rate at which you traced the stars.

**b)** Find the unit rate. Be sure to label the rate with the units of each number.

**c)** What does the unit rate tell you?

**d)** At this rate, how many stars would you trace in 40 seconds? In $2\frac{1}{2}$ minutes?

**3. a)** Write the rate from Question 2a so it compares the number of seconds to the number of stars you traced.

**b)** Find the unit rate. Don't forget to list the units of each number.

**c)** What information does this unit rate tell you?

**d)** At this rate, how long would it take you to trace 25 stars? 75 stars? 100 stars?

**4.** Compare the two unit rates you found in Questions 2 and 3. How are the two rates related? How do you decide which unit rate to use?

**5.** Ryota's tracing rate was 3.5 stars for every 10 seconds, while Sarah's tracing rate was 15 seconds per 4.5 stars. Who is faster at tracing these stars? Explain your reasoning.

 **Wrap It Up**

**MATHEMATICALLY SPEAKING**

▶ rate

▶ unit rate

Two seventh graders, Greg and Richard, tried another experiment where they did jumping jacks. In 10 seconds, Greg finished 17 jumping jacks. What are the two unit rates that can be used to represent his rate? Explain what each unit rate tells you. Richard's jumping jacks per minute rate is less than Greg's. What are some possible rates for Richard?

# On Your Own

Write
About It

1. How does the order of the numbers in a rate affect what the rate means? Use this example: The cost of a dozen bottles of water is $5. Make two different unit rates. Explain what they each mean.

2. Vance and Joyce walk at different rates. Vance walks 7 feet every 2 seconds, while Joyce walks 8 feet every 3 seconds.

   a) Who will travel farther in 1 minute?

   b) If they start at the same place and walk in opposite directions, how far apart will they be after 2 minutes of walking?

3. Karen took a 3-minute typing-speed test and typed 174 words.

   a) Write two different rates based on the results of Karen's test.

   b) Simplify each rate to a unit rate. What does each unit rate tell you?

   c) How long would it take Karen to type a 1,000-word English paper?

   d) How many words can Karen type in $5\frac{1}{2}$ minutes?

4. Some common rates are expressed as single numbers. Rewrite each rate below as a comparison of two numbers.

   a) The unemployment rate is 5.3%.

   b) His heart rate is 64.

   c) The birth rate for the world in 2007 was 20.3.

   **Hint**
   See page 167

5. a) If gasoline costs $3.00 for 1 gallon, how many gallons can you get for $1.00?

   b) If the exchange rate is $1.43 U.S. for 1 euro, how many euros can you get for $1.00 U.S.?

6. Find the cost of 1 item. Round up to the nearest cent.

   a) 1 dozen eggs cost $2.80.

   b) 4 sticks of butter cost $2.29.

   c) 3 T-shirts sell for $19.98.

**7. a)** Sabra runs at a rate of 1 mile in 8 minutes. At this rate, how many miles can Sabra run in 1 hour?

**b)** List three rates that are equivalent to Sabra's speed.

**c)** Jared gave 100 miles in 800 minutes as an equivalent rate. Sabra said, "That's impossible." How can they both be correct?

**d)** Restate Sabra's running rate as miles per 1 minute.

**8.** Fadia went out to dinner for her birthday and had a 16 ounce steak. It cost $30. What was the cost per ounce?

**9. a)** Magazines often offer different subscriptions rates. One weekly magazine had the following offers. Which one would you choose and why?

**$56.94**
26 issues ~~$103.74~~
**You save 45%**

**$79.88**
36 issues ~~$143.64~~
**You save 44%**

**$116.07**
53 issues ~~$211.47~~
**You save 45%**

**b)** What is the weekly cost of this magazine without the discounts?

**10.** Which is the better buy? Explain.

**a)** 10 oz. of trail mix for $1.99 or 15 oz. of trail mix for $2.75

**b)** $92 for 2 pairs of jeans or $141 for 3 pairs of jeans

**11.** The ratio of girls to boys at Camp Encore Coda is 4 : 3. There are 91 campers in all. How many of the campers are boys?

**Think Back**

12. Identify the geometric solid. Indicate the number of faces, edges, vertices and bases.

    **a)**

    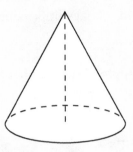

    **b)**

    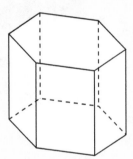

    **c)**

    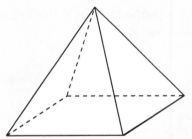

13. Place these fractions in order from least to greatest.

    **a)** $\frac{1}{13}, \frac{1}{10}, \frac{1}{11}$   **b)** $\frac{7}{10}, \frac{7}{6}, \frac{7}{8}$   **c)** $\frac{8}{7}, \frac{8}{5}, \frac{8}{3}$

14. The perimeter of a stop sign is 100 inches. How long is each side? Show your work.

15. Find each product.

    **a)** $-14 \cdot 2.4$

    **b)** $(-1)(-1)^2(-0.01)(-0.1)$

    **c)** $\left(\frac{-3}{4}\right)\left(\frac{12}{39}\right)$

16. Solve for $t$. Show your work.

    $\frac{t}{-12} = 16$

# LESSON 1.4 Proportions

## → Start It Off

1. What words or phrases are used to show rates?

2. Different words are used to mean different operations. If you have $10, which operation would you use to find the amount of money Mary has?

   a) Mary has $4 more than you.

   b) Mary has 4 times as much as you.

   c) Mary has $\frac{1}{4}$ of what you have.

   d) Mary has $4 less than you.

3. Write a comparison question that could be solved using addition or subtraction.

4. Write a comparison question that could be solved using multiplication or division.

# Exploring Proportions

In the general, for every left-handed person, there are 7 right-handed people. There are 581 right-handed students at the John Quincy Adams Middle School.

1. Find the approximate number of left-handed students at John Quincy Adams Middle School. Explain your method.

So far you have used diagrams, ratio tables, and multiplication and division to solve problems involving ratios. You can also solve ratio problems by setting up a proportion. A proportion is an equation that states that two ratios are equal.

The equations below are proportions. They show equal ratios that compare left and right-handed students in a school to the general population. It helps to label what the numbers represent in order to find missing values.

**A.** $\dfrac{\text{left-handed in population}}{\text{right-handed in population}}$ $\dfrac{1}{7} = \dfrac{n}{581}$ $\dfrac{\text{left-handed in school}}{\text{right-handed in school}}$

**B.** $\dfrac{\text{right-handed in population}}{\text{left-handed in population}}$ $\dfrac{7}{1} = \dfrac{581}{n}$ $\dfrac{\text{right-handed in school}}{\text{left-handed in school}}$

**C.** $\dfrac{\text{right-handed in population}}{\text{right-handed in school}}$ $\dfrac{7}{581} = \dfrac{1}{n}$ $\dfrac{\text{left-handed in population}}{\text{left-handed in school}}$

**D.** $\dfrac{\text{right-handed in school}}{\text{right-handed in population}}$ $\dfrac{581}{7} = \dfrac{n}{1}$ $\dfrac{\text{left-handed in school}}{\text{left-handed in population}}$

**2.** **a)** What do you notice about the proportions?

**b)** Which ratios compare people in the general population to the students in the school?

**c)** Which ratios compare the number of right-handers to the number of left-handers?

**d)** How are the different proportions similar?

When working with proportions, the term cross products is often used. The word *cross* tells us to look at the pairs of numbers diagonally across from each other in a proportion. The word *product* indicates multiplication, so take these numbers and multiply them together.

$$\frac{1}{7} = \frac{83}{581}$$

$$\frac{1}{7} = \frac{83}{581}$$

The cross products equal 581, $1 \cdot 581$ and $7 \cdot 83$.

The next example asks you to examine three relationships found in proportions.

A snack mix uses 16 ounces of peanuts for every 10 ounces of raisins. Another snack mix uses 72 ounces of peanuts for every 45 ounces of raisins. Show that the ratios 16 to 10 and 72 to 45 represent the same relationship between the number of ounces of peanuts and the number of ounces of raisins.

**Proportion**

$$\frac{16}{10} = \frac{72}{45} \qquad \text{Number ounces peanuts}$$
$$\text{Number ounces raisins}$$

**Relationship 1:** Both ratios in a proportion simplify to the same ratio.

Each ratio simplifies to 8 ounces of peanuts for every 5 ounces of raisins.

Divide both 16 and 10 by 2, or multiply both 16 and 10 by $\frac{1}{2}$.

Divide both 72 and 45 by 9, or multiply both 72 and 45 by $\frac{1}{9}$.

$$\frac{16 \div 2}{10 \div 2} = \frac{8}{5} \qquad \frac{16 \cdot \frac{1}{2}}{10 \cdot \frac{1}{2}} = \frac{8}{5} \qquad \frac{72 \div 9}{45 \div 9} = \frac{8}{5} \qquad \frac{72 \cdot \frac{1}{9}}{45 \cdot \frac{1}{9}} = \frac{8}{5}$$

**Relationship 2:** Both ratios in a proportion have the same value.

The value of both of the ratios is 1.6.

$$16 \div 10 = 1.6 \qquad 72 \div 45 = 1.6$$

**Relationship 3:** The cross products in a proportion are equal.

The cross products in the proportion each equal 720.

$$10 \cdot 72 = 720$$

$$\frac{16}{10} = \frac{72}{45}$$

$$16 \cdot 45 = 720$$

3.  Check to see if the three relationships in the Example hold for these proportions. Show your work.

   **a)**  $60:12 = 15:3$

   **b)**  $\frac{4}{6} = \frac{6}{9}$

   **c)**  $\frac{3}{5} = \frac{5}{8.34}$

**4.** Show that the three relationships do not hold for these pairs of ratios, which are not equal.

**a)** $\frac{7}{14} \neq \frac{1}{3}$

**b)** $8:5 \neq 24:6$

**c)** $\frac{9}{4} \neq \frac{36}{18}$

**5.** Examine the last relationship in the Example. Why are the cross products in a proportion equal?

MATHEMATICALLY SPEAKING

▶ proportional

Have you heard the word proportional? What does this word mean? How is it related to proportions? Let's investigate.

The table below shows the cost of purchasing notebooks. In any column, if you divide the total cost of the notebooks by the number of notebooks, you get the same number. We say that the total cost of the notebooks "is proportional to" the number of notebooks purchased.

| Cost of Notebooks (a) | $3.99 | $7.98 | $11.97 | $15.96 | $19.95 |
|---|---|---|---|---|---|
| Number of Notebooks (b) | 1 | 2 | 3 | 4 | 5 |

If $a$ and $b$ are variables representing two quantities, then "$a$ is proportional to $b$" means that the relationship between $a$ and $b$ is multiplicative. So, ratios of pairs of related values of $a$ and $b$ are equivalent. For example, the ratio 1 notebook for $3.99 is equivalent to the ratio 3 notebooks for $12.97.

**6. a)** Jane ran 1 mile in 7 minutes. Later, Jane found that it takes her 15 minutes to run 2 miles. Is the number of miles Jane runs proportional to the amount of time it takes her to run the distance? Why or why not?

**b)** Emily formed the following ratio table. Is $a$ proportional to $b$? If so, why? If not, why not?

| a | 12 | 6 | 3 | 1.2 |
|---|---|---|---|---|
| b | 10 | 5 | 2.5 | 1 |

**c)** Describe the relationship in b) between $a$ and $b$ using an equation.

**d)** Create a table of two quantities, $a$ and $b$, where $a$ is proportional to $b$.

# Using Proportions to Solve Problems

You can now solve proportional problems when one value is unknown.

## Example

The ratio of ounces of peanuts to raisins in a snack mix was $72 : 45$. You have 20 ounces of raisins and want to add peanuts. How many ounces of peanuts should you use to keep the same proportion of peanuts to raisins?

**Method 1:** Simplify one ratio. Set up a proportion and solve it by scaling the ratio up or down.

$$\frac{72}{45} = \frac{\cancel{72}^{8}}{\cancel{45}_{5}} = \frac{8}{5}$$

Simplify $\frac{72}{45}$ by dividing both numbers by 9.

$$\frac{\text{peanuts}}{\text{raisins}} \quad \overset{\times\,4}{\underset{\times\,4}{\frac{8}{5} = \frac{n}{20}}}$$

Scale $\frac{8}{5}$ up by multiplying both numerator and denominator by 4. $n = 32$

32 ounces of peanuts are needed.

**Method 2:** Set up a proportion and solve it using the value of one ratio.

$$\frac{\text{peanuts}}{\text{raisins}} \quad \frac{72}{45} = \frac{n}{20}$$

Set up a proportion.

$$1.6 = \frac{n}{20}$$

Find the value of the ratio ($72 \div 45$).

$$20 \cdot 1.6 = \frac{n}{20} \cdot 20$$

Solve the equation by multiplying each side by 20.

$$32 = n$$

32 ounces of peanuts are needed.

**Method 3:** Set up a proportion and solve it using cross products.

$$\frac{\text{peanuts}}{\text{raisins}} \quad \frac{72}{45} = \frac{n}{20}$$

Set up a proportion.

$$72 \cdot 20 = 45 \cdot n$$

Set cross products equal to each other.

$$1{,}440 = 45n$$

Multiply.

$$1{,}440 \div 45 = n$$

Divide.

$$32 = n$$

32 ounces of peanuts are needed.

7. At a diner, six eggs are used to make 4 omelets. How many eggs are needed for 30 omelets? Explain in your own words how to use the three methods described in the example to solve this problem.

8. For each problem, write a proportion. Solve for the unknown value using one of the three methods for solving proportions.

a) An average person burns 30 calories every 5 minutes when skating. How many calories does an average person use if she skates for 45 minutes?

b) After playing basketball for 60 minutes, Arjun used 450 calories. How much longer should he play basketball if he wants to use 500 calories?

c) The average soccer player uses 78 calories every 10 minutes. How many calories will a player use in a game that lasts 52 minutes?

d) An eraser and a pencil are on a desk. You can see the length of the eraser when it is measured using beads.

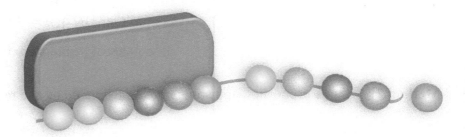

Using paperclips to measure the length of the eraser and pencil, you find that:

The eraser is four paperclips long.
The pencil is six paperclips long.

How long is the pencil in beads?

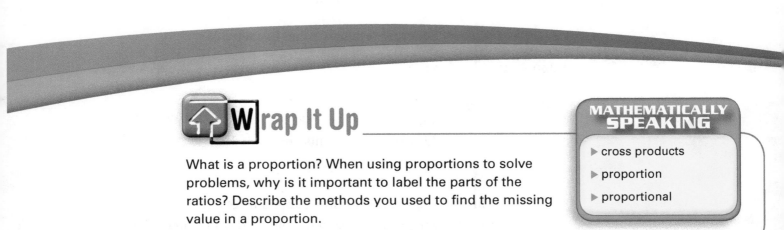

## Wrap It Up

What is a proportion? When using proportions to solve problems, why is it important to label the parts of the ratios? Describe the methods you used to find the missing value in a proportion.

MATHEMATICALLY SPEAKING

▶ cross products
▶ proportion
▶ proportional

Write
About It

1. Describe all the relationships between the two ratios in $\frac{6}{8} = \frac{18}{24}$.

2. In a recipe for corn bread, the ratio of milk to flour is $\frac{1}{2}:1\frac{1}{2}$. The school cafeteria is making a huge batch of corn bread. How much milk is needed if 21 cups of flour are used?

3. A batch of coleslaw uses $1\frac{1}{2}$ cups of chopped cabbage for every $\frac{2}{3}$ cup of grated carrots. After chopping a cabbage, Mrs. Winslow finds she has 9 cups. How many cups of carrots does she need to make a batch of coleslaw?

4. A Boeing 747 traveled 2,464 air miles from New York City to Los Angeles in $5\frac{1}{2}$ hours. How long will it take the aircraft to make the 719-mile trip from New York City to Chicago?

5. Most people blink their eyes 20 times per minute. How many blinks happen in 12 seconds?

6. Determine if these ratios are equivalent and can be written as a proportion.

    a) $\frac{45}{9}, \frac{10}{2}$

    b) $\frac{40}{12}, \frac{95}{8}$

    c) $\frac{8}{18}, \frac{20}{45}$

7. A flower shop sells bouquets that use roses and carnations in a ratio of 4 to 5. The shop just bought 343 carnations. How many roses will they need to make the bouquets? How many bouquets will they be able to make?

8. Two popular cola brands often hold blind taste tests. *Consumer Reports* found that with regular cola drinkers, only 7 out of 19 people could pick out their favorite brand of cola.

    a) A taste test was done with 100 cola drinkers. How many would be able to tell the difference between the two major colas? Round to the nearest person.

    b) Another taste test was done with 250 people. How many people would not be able to tell the difference between the two major colas? Round to the nearest person.

9. Orange paint is made by mixing red and yellow paint in a ratio of 4 to 5. A school is painting its hallways and needs 315 gallons of orange paint. How many gallons of red paint and yellow paint should be ordered?

10. A middle school principal tries to keep the number of students in each homeroom under 25. She also tries to keep the boy-girl ratio at 50%. In Room 203 there are 9 boys and 17 girls. In Room 205 there are 10 boys and 15 girls.

    a) Which homeroom has the ratio of boys to girls closest to 50%?

    b) A new female student has just enrolled. Which homeroom should she be assigned to? Explain.

11. Elizabeth lives in New Mexico. She is going to Europe and wants to change $100 into euros. The exchange rate is 1 euro for $1.4660. How many euros will she get for her $100?

12. A pancake mix recipe calls for 2 cups of mix to make 15 pancakes. If you only want to make 10 pancakes, how many cups of mix are needed?

13. The length of a rectangle is twice its width. If the perimeter of the rectangle is 54 cm, find its length and width.

14. What does, "The amount of green paint is proportional to the amount of yellow paint in this lime-colored mixture" mean?

15. Use cross products to find $n$.

    a) $\left(\frac{3}{4}\right):12 = n:32$

    b) $n:\left(\frac{2}{5}\right) = \frac{1}{4}:\left(\frac{7}{10}\right)$

    c) $\frac{19}{3} = \frac{14}{n}$

16. Write the value of one ratio and then find $n$.

    a) $\frac{n}{5} = \frac{27}{12}$

    b) $37:10 = n:0.61$

    c) $\frac{3}{n} = \frac{16}{20}$

**17.** Simplify one ratio and then scale it up or down to find $n$.

a) $\frac{56}{n} = \frac{32}{48}$

b) $\frac{28}{49} = \frac{n}{14}$

c) $4:35 = n:525$

 **Think Beyond**

**18.** Java Coffee Shop blends coffee using a ratio of 3 parts Columbian beans to 2 parts Kenyan beans to 1 part Kona beans. The employees need to make 324 pounds of this coffee blend. They sell the coffee blend for $12.99 per pound. But the beans cost much less—$3.42 per pound for Columbian, $2.88 per pound for Kenyan and $4.00 per pound for Kona. What is the profit on the 324 pounds of coffee sold?

 **Think Back**

**19.** Write these numbers in standard form.

a) one billion, forty-nine thousand, two and seven hundred five ten-thousandths

b) sixty-three trillion, four hundred million, ninety thousand and twelve thousandths

c) eight million and eight millionths

**20.** Graph the set of ordered pairs $(x, y)$ such that $x$ is an integer between $-3$ and $2$ and $y = -1$.

**21.** The greatest common factor of two numbers is 4. The least common multiple of the same two numbers is 60. If one of the numbers is 20, what is the other number?

**22.** Find the difference. Show your work.

a) $\frac{6}{7} - \frac{1}{8}$

b) $-\frac{10}{12} - \frac{5}{6}$

**23.** Write the following fractions as decimals. Show your work.

a) $\frac{5}{12}$

b) $\frac{14}{20}$

c) $4\frac{9}{25}$

# Proportional Relationships

## Start It Off

Two friends are making orange juice by mixing orange concentrate and water. They each made a different mixture.

| Mixture A | Mixture B |
|---|---|
| 5 cups of water | 6 cups of water |
| 3 cups of orange concentrate | 4 cups of orange concentrate |

1. Which drink will taste the orangiest? Explain.

2. What ratio of concentrate to water will taste orangier than both mixtures?

## Equations of Proportional Relationships

In Lesson 1.4, you investigated proportions. Now you will learn how to write equations of proportional relationships.

1. Think about what happens to a square's perimeter when the length of the square's side changes. Copy and complete the table below.

| Length of Side (cm) | 1 | 2 | 3 | 4 | 5 | 6 |
|---|---|---|---|---|---|---|
| Perimeter (cm) | 4 | | | | | |

2. a) Why is the relationship between the perimeter and the side length of a square proportional?

   b) Write a sentence that compares the perimeter to the side length of any square.

   c) Let $x$ represent the side length of a square and $y$ represent its perimeter. Write an equation that relates $x$ and $y$.

When $y$ is proportional to $x$, the quotient $y \div x$ is the value of their ratio. This number does not change when different corresponding values of $x$ and $y$ are used. In other words, the value of the ratio $\frac{y}{x}$ is fixed, or constant. The relationship between $y$ and $x$ can be expressed using the equation:

$$y = \text{fixed value} \cdot x$$

This fixed value is also known as the constant of proportionality.

**Example**

Carol bought a fish tank and plans to stock it with fish. The pet store recommends keeping the ratio of angelfish to guppies at 2 to 7. Write an equation that Carol can use that relates the number of guppies, $g$, to the number of angelfish, $a$.

**Step 1:** Write and label the ratio that relates the *number of guppies* to the *number of angelfish*.

$$\frac{\text{number of guppies}}{\text{number of angelfish}} \qquad \frac{7}{2}$$

**Step 2:** Find the fixed value of the ratio by dividing: $7 \div 2 = 3.5$.

**Step 3:** Write the equation that relates the number of guppies and angelfish using the fixed value.

$$g = 3.5a \qquad \text{or} \qquad g = \frac{7}{2}a$$

3. **a)** Write an equation that relates *the number of angelfish* to *the number of guppies*. Follow the steps above.

   **b)** Why are there two possible equations for most proportional relationships?

4. Create a proportional situation for which you can write only one equation. Find the equation.

5. The highway distance traveled in a car is proportional to the number of gallons used by the car. Wayne traveled 407 miles and used 11 gallons of gasoline. His brother drove 520 miles and used 13 gallons.

   a) Write a proportion for each car that compares the distance traveled, $y$, to the number of gallons of gasoline used, $x$.

   b) Write an equation for each car that compares the distance traveled, $y$, to the number of gallons of gasoline used, $x$. Use the proportions in Part a to help you.

   c) Which car gets more miles per gallon of gasoline?

   d) What does the value of the ratio in each equation tell you?

6. The cost of advertising on the radio is proportional to the length of time the ad is aired. One station charges $37 for every 30 seconds. Write an equation that relates the number of seconds to the cost of the ad. Let $d$ represent number of dollars and $s$ represent number of seconds.

# Graphs of Proportional Relationships

 Vegetables can grow to be enormous. Many state fairs host competitions to see who can grow the heaviest pumpkin, the tallest stalk of okra or the longest green bean. Depending on where the vegetable was grown, weights are reported in kilograms or in pounds. Examine the table of record weights below.

| Vegetable | Weight (kilograms) | Weight (pounds) | Ratio of Pounds to Kilograms |
|---|---|---|---|
| Squash | 30 | 66 | |
| Radish | 10 | 22 | |
| Carrot | 2 | 4.4 | |
| Tomato | 3.17 | 7 | |
| Zucchini | 25 | 55 | |
| Turnip | 9.52 | 21 | |
| Brussels sprout | 5 | 11 | |

7. **a)** Copy the table and fill in the last column for each vegetable.

   **b)** Are the ratios equivalent? How did you decide?

   **c)** Is the relationship that relates pounds and kilograms a proportional relationship? Why or why not?

   **d)** Write an equation that relates the number of pounds to the number of kilograms.

8. Below is a graph of the data from the table above.

   **a)** Which quadrant is the graph in?

   **b)** Give a title for the graph.

   **c)** Describe the scale.

   **d)** Explain what the point (25, 55) represents on the graph.

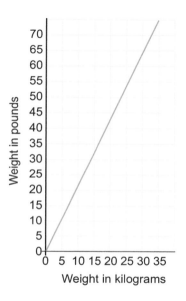

9. **a)** Use the graph to fill in the table:

| | Vegetable | Weight (kilograms) | Weight (pounds) |
|---|---|---|---|
| **i)** | cauliflower | 7 | |
| **ii)** | celery | | 35 |
| **iii)** | sweet potato | 20 | |

   **b)** Use the equation from Question 7 to find the weights of the vegetables in Part a.

   **c)** Why is it better in this situation to use an equation instead of a graph to determine the weights?

10. **a)** Rodney thinks the graph shows equivalent ratios. Do you agree or disagree with Rodney?

   **b)** Tom thinks the graph can be used to convert kilograms to pounds or pounds to kilograms. Ella disagrees. Who's correct? Explain.

# Direct Variation

Graphs of proportional relationships have a few things in common. Sketch the following graphs.

$$y = 3x \qquad\qquad y = \frac{1}{2}x \qquad\qquad y = x$$

**11.** What are two things all three graphs have in common?

**12. a)** What is the value of the constant ratio in each of the equations above?

**b)** Make a table of six $x$- and $y$-values for each equation. Write a ratio to compare $y:x$ for each ordered pair. Find the value of the ratio.

**c)** Explain how the value of the ratio $y:x$ affects the steepness of the line when graphed.

**MATHEMATICALLY SPEAKING**

▶ direct proportion

▶ direct variation

We call a relationship between two quantities in which the ratio remains constant a direct proportion, or direct variation. Graphs of direct proportions are straight lines that go through the origin. Not all straight-line graphs represent direct proportional relationships.

---

**Example**

**Direct Variation**

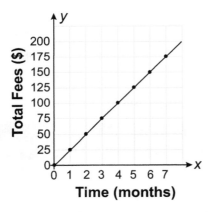

Total Fees ($)

Time (months)

**Not Direct Variation**

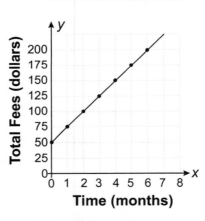

Total Fees (dollars)

Time (months)

In a direct variation or direct proportion relationship, the ratio between total fees and time $(25:1)$ remains constant for all ordered pairs.

**13.** **a)** Find the ratio of cost to distance traveled for each coordinate pair in the table.

**b)** Is the relationship between cost and distance traveled proportional?

**c)** Why or why not?

 **rap It Up**

What does it mean for *y* to be proportional to *x*? How are proportional relationships expressed in tables, in equations and in graphs? Give examples.

**MATHEMATICALLY SPEAKING**

▶ constant

▶ constant of proportionality

▶ direct proportion

▶ direct variation

▶ fixed value

**Write About It**

1. Crystal runs 5 kilometers in 20 minutes. Make four equivalent rates that describe her running rate. Graph the rates on a coordinate grid with time on the $x$-axis and distance on the $y$-axis. Describe the graph and write the equation of the line.

2. A regular octagon has a side length of $x$ cm. Write an equation to find the perimeter, $y$, of the octagon.

3. a) The cost of a deli sandwich is $3.49. Write an equation to find the cost, $y$, of $x$ sandwiches.

   b) What types of numbers can you use for $x$?

4. Tim's mom is 39 years old and Tim is 13 years old. Next year his mom will be 40 years old and Tim will be 14 years old. The following year they will be 41 and 15 respectively.

   a) Are Tim's and his mother's ages proportional? Why or why not?

   b) How old was Tim's mom when Tim was born?

   c) Write an equation that compares Tim's age, $x$, to his mom's age, $y$.

5. Regina traced 7.5 stars in 30 seconds.

   a) Find equivalent rates for the number of stars Regina traced in 10, 20, 40, 50 and 60 seconds.

   b) Write an equation that represents the number of stars, $y$, that Regina can draw in $x$ seconds.

   c) Where is Regina's unit rate shown in the equation?

   d) Draw Quadrant I of the coordinate plane. Label the $x$-axis "Time in Seconds" and the $y$-axis "Number of Stars." Plot the equivalent rates as coordinate points (time in seconds, number of stars).

Examine the tables in Questions 6 and 7. Answer the following questions for both.

**a)** Is the relationship between $x$ and $y$ proportional? Why or why not?

**b)** Write an equation that describes each relationship.

**6.**

| x | y |
|---|---|
| 7 | 21 |
| 18 | 54 |
| $\frac{2}{3}$ | 2 |
| 4.1 | 12.3 |
| 2 | 6 |
| −3 | −9 |

**7.**

| x | y |
|---|---|
| 0 | 3 |
| 1 | 5 |
| 2 | 7 |
| 3 | 9 |
| 4 | 11 |
| 5 | 13 |

**8.** The number of books in the Edison Library is 1,134 less than the number of books in the King Library. Write an equation relating the number of books in each library. Let $e$ represent number of books in Edison Library and $k$ represent number of books in King Library. Is this a proportional relationship?

**9.** At a fruit stand, 5 peaches are sold for $3.00. Write an equation to find the cost, $c$, of $p$ peaches.

Aaron and Lily participated in a 20-mile Walk Against Hunger event. Both walked at a steady pace, but Aaron walked faster and finished before Lily. Use the graph below to answer Questions 10 and 11.

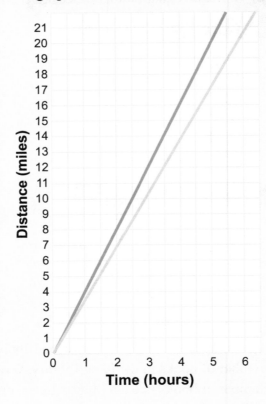

**10. a)** Which of the two lines represents Aaron's walking rate? Explain.

**b)** List three points on this line. What do they represent?

**c)** Find the equation of the line that represents Aaron's walking rate.

**11. a)** How long did it take Lily to walk 20 miles? 14 miles? 7 miles? 1 mile?

**b)** Is the relationship between distance walked and time proportional? How can you tell?

**c)** Find the equation of the line that represents Lily's walking rate.

Questions 12–16 refer to the same situation.

**12.** Leslie applied for a job at a gas station. The owner said she could earn $264 for $5\frac{1}{2}$ days of work.

    **a)** How much money does she earn in 1 day? In 2 days?

    **b)** Leslie works 8 hours a day. How much does she earn per hour?

**13.** Below is a graph of Leslie's earning rate.

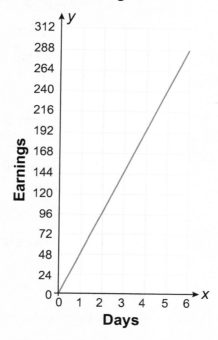

    **a)** How can you use the graph to find the amount of money Leslie will earn in 3 days?

    **b)** Why does the graph go through the origin?

    **c)** Do the graphs of proportional situations always go through the origin? Explain.

    **d)** Write the equation of this line.

**14.** Leslie decides to look for another job. She finds one that pays $350 for 7 8-hour days of work. Is this a better-paying job? Explain.

**15.** Leslie hopes to find a job where she earns $8 per hour for an 8-hour day.

    **a)** Write an equation for her earnings based on the number of days she works.

    **b)** Draw a graph that shows Leslie's earnings at this rate of pay for up to 5 days.

**Think Beyond**

16. Leslie found a different job. On Day 1 she received $1 for the day. On Day 2 the rate doubled and she earned $2 for the day. On Day 3 the previous day's wages were doubled and she received $4. On Day 4 the daily rate again doubled the previous day's rate and she was paid $8.

   a) Continuing with this salary, how much will Leslie have earned on the 20th day of work?

   b) What will the sum of her wages on Days 1–20 be?

   c) Is the relationship between salary and number of days proportional? Why or why not?

   d) Graph Leslie's salary with the number of days on the *x*-axis and the daily earnings on the *y*-axis for 9 days.

**Think Back**

17. Harvey buys a couch for $798.99, an ottoman for $449.99 and an LCD TV for $689.99.

   a) Estimate the total cost of the three items.

   b) Estimate the amount of sales tax Harvey will pay if the sales tax rate is 5%.

18. Choose the phrase that best matches the equation $5b = e - 13$.

   A. Five times the amount that Betty makes is the same as thirteen dollars less then what Estelle makes.

   B. Betty makes thirteen dollars less than five times the amount that Estelle makes.

   C. Five times the amount that Betty makes minus thirteen dollars is the same as the amount that Estelle makes.

19. Solve for *n*. Check the solution. $^-8 - n = 0$

20. Find the missing addend to complete each true statement.

   a) $\frac{1}{8} + \frac{\square}{\square} = \frac{3}{8} + \frac{1}{4}$     c) $\frac{\square}{\square} + \frac{6}{5} = \frac{3}{10} + \frac{17}{10}$

   b) $\frac{2}{6} + \frac{2}{3} = \frac{3}{6} + \frac{\square}{\square}$     d) $\frac{3}{4} + \frac{7}{4} = \frac{\square}{\square} + 2$

21. *Emirps* are numbers that are prime when read forward and backward. For example, the number 13 is an emirp because 31 is also prime. Name three different emirp pairs.

**Optional Technology Lesson for this section available in your eBook**

# SECTION 1

# Sum It Up

## Ratios and Rates

▪ Ratios compare two or more quantities multiplicatively.

In a recipe, the amount of sugar to the amount of flour is in a ratio of $2:5$.

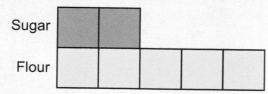

There are $\frac{2}{5}$ times as many cups of sugar as cups of flour. There are $\frac{5}{2}$ times as many cups of flour as cups of sugar.

▪ A rate is a type of ratio that compares different types of measures. A unit rate is a rate in which the second number in the ratio is 1.

▪ Equivalent ratios and rates have the same value.

$$1:3 = 1 \div 3 = \frac{1}{3} \text{ or } 0.\overline{3} \qquad 4:12 = 4 \div 12 = \frac{1}{3} \text{ or } 0.\overline{3} \qquad 16:48 = 16 \div 48 = \frac{1}{3} \text{ or } 0.\overline{3}$$

## Proportions

- A proportion is an equation that shows that two ratios are equal.

- The values of the ratios in a proportion are equal: $\frac{72}{45} = \frac{16}{10}$

  $\frac{72}{45} = 72 \div 45 = 1.6$        $\frac{16}{10} = 16 \div 10 = 1.6$

- Numbers in a proportion are related by multiplication and division. You can scale up or scale down a ratio to form an equivalent ratio.

$$\frac{72}{45} = \frac{16}{10} \qquad \overset{\div\,4.5}{\underset{\div\,4.5}{\frac{72}{45} = \frac{16}{10}}} \qquad \overset{\times\,4.5}{\underset{\times\,4.5}{\frac{72}{45} = \frac{16}{10}}}$$

- The cross products in a proportion are equal.

  $\frac{72}{45} = \frac{16}{10}$

  $72 \cdot 10 = 45 \cdot 16$

  $720 = 720$

- When $a$ is proportional to $b$, the quotient of $a \div b$ is the fixed value of the ratio. The fixed value of the ratio is also known as the constant of proportionality.

- Proportional relationships can be expressed in many ways. For example, the cost to buy pencils is proportional to the number of pencils purchased. The rate of 10¢ per pencil is shown in the table. The ratio of cost to number of pencils is a constant ratio, equivalent to $y:x$.

| Number of Pencils ($x$) | Cost in Cents ($y$) |
|:---:|:---:|
| 0 | 0 |
| 1 | 10 |
| 2 | 20 |
| 3 | 30 |
| 4 | 40 |
| 5 | 50 |
| 6 | 60 |

■ The graph of this relationship, and all proportional relationships, is a straight line through the origin. The equation of a proportional relationship is in the form $y$ = fixed value (of a proportional relationship) $\cdot x$, and in this case $y = 10x$.

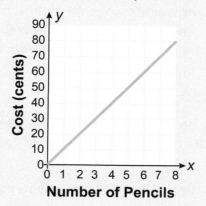

**Number of Pencils**

## MATHEMATICALLY SPEAKING

Do you know what these mathematical terms mean?

▶ constant

▶ constant of proportionality

▶ cross products

▶ direct proportion

▶ direct variation

▶ equivalent ratios

▶ fixed value

▶ multiplicative comparison

▶ part-to-part ratio

▶ part-to-whole ratio

▶ proportion

▶ proportional

▶ rate

▶ ratio

▶ simplified ratio

▶ unit rate

▶ value of a ratio

# Study Guide

**Comparing Quantities**

## Part 1. What did you learn?

1. Katie made a design using triangle and trapezoid pattern blocks. She said, "The value for the triangle-to-trapezoid ratio is 0.75." Use this information to fill in the blanks below. Use whole numbers only.

   a. The ratio of triangles to trapezoids is _____ to _____.

   b. If Katie uses 24 triangles in her design, she needs to use _____ trapezoids so that the triangles and trapezoids are in proportion.

   c. If Katie uses a total of 70 pattern blocks, she needs to use _____ triangles and _____ trapezoids to keep the same triangle-to-trapezoid ratio of 0.75.

2. Find the missing value in the diagram below. Each square represents the same value.

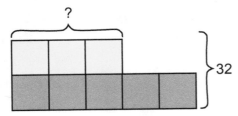

3. Lara weighs packages for an express delivery company. One customer came in with two packages. Package A is $\frac{4}{9}$ the weight of Package B.

   a. Give three possible weights for Package A and three possible weights for Package B.

   b. What does the statement, "Package A is $\frac{4}{9}$ the weight of Package B" mean?

   c. What is the ratio of the weight of Package A to the weight of Package B?

   d. What is the ratio of the weight of Package B to the weight of Package A?

   e. Write a multiplication sentence that compares the weight of Package B to the weight of Package A.

4. Deidre and Eric each collect coins. One day they compared the number of quarters, the number of dimes and the number of nickels they each had. Copy and complete the following chart.

| | I. Type of Coin | II. Ratio of the Number of Deidre's Coins to the Number of Eric's Coins | III. Diagram of the Number of Deidre's Coins to the Number of Eric's Coins | IV. Comparison Sentence that Expresses the Number of Deidre's Coins as a Faction of the Number of Eric's Coins. |
|---|---|---|---|---|
| a. | quarter | | | Deidre has $\frac{2}{3}$ as many quarters as Eric. |
| b. | dime | 1 : 2 | | |
| c. | nickel | | | |

5. Samara makes her own salad dressing. She uses $\frac{2}{3}$ cup vinegar for every $1\frac{1}{3}$ cups oil. If Samara makes 4 cups of dressing, how many cups of vinegar and how many cups of oil does she need?

6. Use the cross product method to find the value of $n$ in the proportion $\frac{10}{5} = \frac{n}{1.5}$.

7. Write the ratio $\frac{3}{2}$ as a single number value and then use an equation to find the value of $n$ in the proportion $\frac{3}{2} = \frac{n}{12}$.

8. Find the value of $n$ in the proportion $\frac{3}{8} = \frac{21}{n}$ by scaling the ratio up or down.

9. At Lee's supermarket, 2.5 pounds of bananas cost $5.00. Write two different unit rates relating the weight and price of bananas. Label each unit rate.

10. Littletown Public Library charges a fine for each day a book is overdue. The coordinate graph below shows data about the relationship between the number of days a book is overdue and the cost of the fine.

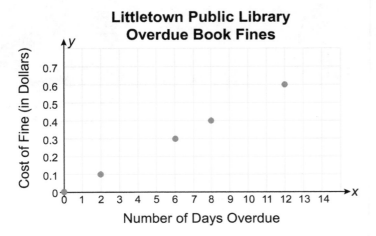

**Littletown Public Library Overdue Book Fines**

a. Use the coordinate graph to copy and complete the table below.

| Number of Days | 0 | 1 | 2 | 3 | 4 | 5 | 6 | 7 | 8 |
|---|---|---|---|---|---|---|---|---|---|
| Overdue Fine | | | | | | | | | |

b. Explain why the relationship between number of days and cost of the overdue fine is proportional.

c. Find the constant of proportionality between the number of days and the cost of the overdue fine.

d. Why is this type of relation between two quantities called a direct variation?

e. Write an equation that relates $x$, number of days a book is overdue, to $y$, the total cost of the overdue fine.

f. What is the fine for a book that is 14 days overdue?

g. If the fine is $1.50, for how many days is the book overdue?

**11.** Nathan was asked the following multiple-choice question on a recent quiz.

> The ratio of waiters to customers at Hola restaurant is 2:5. What is the single number value for the waiter-to-customer ratio?
>
> **A.** 0.4          **C.** 2.5
>
> **B.** 2             **D.** 5

Nathan chose letter C because "$5 \div 2 = 2.5$." What is wrong with Nathan's reasoning? What could you say or do to help him find and fix his error?

**12.** Olive's teacher asked her to calculate the price per pound of bananas if 3 pounds cost $1.50. Olive wrote, "The price is $2 because $3.00 \div \$1.50 = \$2$." Olive's teacher told her that her answer was incorrect. Why? What is wrong with Olive's reasoning? What could you say or do to help her find and fix her error?

# Scaling Up and Down

Scale models and drawings are used by engineers when designing cars and aircraft, by artists when creating miniatures or large sculptures, and by scientists when representing microscopic creatures and plants. Enlargements and reductions are similar to the original objects. In this section, you will learn how ratios are used to produce scale drawings and similar figures.

**LESSON 2.1 Scale Drawings**

 **Start It Off**

1. Express these fractions as percents.

   **a)** $\frac{1}{4}, \frac{1}{2}, \frac{3}{4}, 1$

   **b)** $\frac{1}{5}, \frac{2}{5}, \frac{3}{5}, \frac{4}{5}, \frac{5}{5}$

2. Describe a quick method of converting any number of fifths to a percent.

3. Yolanda uses her knowledge that $\frac{1}{8}$ is half of $\frac{1}{4}$ to remember the percent value for $\frac{1}{8}$. What do you think she does?

4. **a)** Give the percent values for $\frac{1}{8}, \frac{2}{8}, \frac{3}{8}, \frac{4}{8}, \frac{5}{8}, \frac{6}{8}$ and $\frac{7}{8}$.

   **b)** Describe mental strategies you can use to determine the percent values of $\frac{3}{8}, \frac{6}{8}$ and $\frac{7}{8}$.

# Understanding Scale

**MATHEMATICALLY SPEAKING**

▶ scale drawing

▶ scale

▶ linear dimension

What do you think of when someone uses the word *scale*? Musical scales? A pay scale? A scale for comparing weights?

A scale drawing is a drawing that represents a real object. Maps are a common type of scale drawing.

**1.** Describe three jobs or situations where scale drawings are used. Why is having a scale drawing important in each situation?

A scale drawing is made to a specific ratio that relates each linear measurement of the scale drawing to the corresponding linear measurement of the real object. This ratio is called the scale of the drawing. A scale is usually expressed in one of two ways:

- using units, as in 1 cm to 1 m

- without mentioning units, as in 1:100

If no units are included, both numbers in the ratio have the same unit. For example, a scale of 1:100 can represent 1 centimeter to 100 centimeters or 1 kilometer to 100 kilometers, but would not represent 1 centimeter to 100 kilometers.

The first number in a scale always refers to a length on the scale drawing and the second number refers to the corresponding length on the original object. When the scale is 1 to 100, you can say that each dimension on the scale drawing is 100 times as short as the corresponding dimension of the actual object or that each dimension of the object is 100 times as long as the corresponding dimension on the scale drawing.

**2.** Scale drawings are made using the following scales. Tell what each scale means. If no units are given, provide reasonable ones.

**a)** Drawing of basketball court; scale of 1:20

**b)** Drawing of a tree frog; scale of 3:1

**c)** Floor plan of your school; scale of $\frac{1}{4}$ inch for every 1 foot

**3. a)** Rewrite the scale in Problem 2c so the units are the same.

**b)** Give three different equivalent ratios for the scale in Problem 2c.

To determine the scale, compare the same linear dimension on both the scale drawing and the original. Scales are easier to understand if you simplify the ratio so the second number in the ratio is 1 or if you find the value of the ratio.

What scale was used to create the drawing of the nutrition bar?

**Step 1:** Write a ratio comparing the same linear dimension on the scale drawing and the original bar.

$$\frac{2.5}{10}$$

**Step 2:** Simplify the ratio or find the value of the ratio.

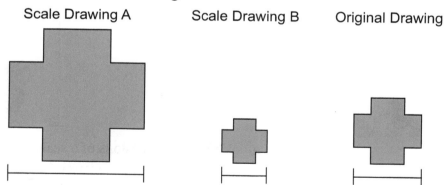

Value of ratio: $2.5 \div 10 = \frac{1}{4}$

The scale is 1 to 4, which can be expressed as $\frac{1}{4}$ or 0.25. The scale drawing of the nutrition bar is $\frac{1}{4}$ as long and $\frac{1}{4}$ as wide as the original nutrition bar. Notice that the scale drawing is smaller than the original bar.

**4.** Examine the scale drawings below.

Scale Drawing A          Scale Drawing B          Original Drawing

**a)** Compare Drawing A and the original drawing by using linear dimensions to find the scale.

**b)** Compare Drawing B and the original drawing by using linear dimensions to find the scale.

**c)** Gloriana said, "I think the scale for creating Drawing A is 4 to 1. It looks like four copies of the original design will fit into the larger one." But the scale for Drawing A is not 4 to 1. Why is Gloriana confused? What might you say to help her?

**5.** Examine the drawings in Question 4.

   **a)** If Drawing B were the original drawing, what would be the scale for Drawing A?

   **b)** If Drawing A were the original drawing, what would be the scale for Drawing B?

   **c)** What does the order of the numbers in a ratio indicate about a scale drawing? Explain.

**6.** Books and Internet websites often use scale drawings. Use the ratios and lengths in each scale drawing to calculate the actual length or height of the creature in centimeters.

   **a)** Puffin, scale of 1:10

   **b)** Albatross, scale of 1:38

   **c)** Planaria, scale of 8:1

**MATHEMATICALLY SPEAKING**

▶ enlargement

▶ reduction

**7. a)** When the dimensions of a scale drawing are greater than the corresponding dimensions of an object, the scale drawing is called an enlargement. Which of the scale drawings in Question 6 are enlargements? What do you notice about the scale?

   **b)** When the dimensions of a scale drawing are less than the corresponding dimensions of an object, the scale drawing is called a reduction. Which of the scale drawings in Question 6 are reductions? What do you notice about the scale?

   **c)** What is the scale when the scale drawing is the same size as the original object?

# Making a Scale Drawing

Architects and designers use scale drawings called blueprints to plan their work. This blueprint is of a one-bedroom apartment.

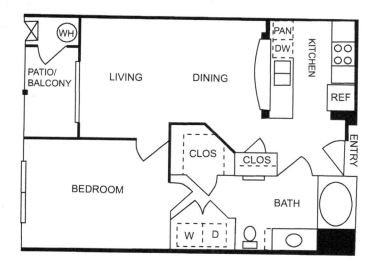

8. **a)** What are the dimensions of the scale drawing in inches?

   **b)** The scale of the blueprint is 1 to 105. What are the dimensions of the actual apartment in feet?

9. A different one-bedroom apartment is 32 feet by 20 feet. The apartment is in the shape of a rectangle.

   **a)** Design the layout of the apartment and make a scale drawing of it on grid paper. Use $\frac{1}{4}$-inch, $\frac{1}{2}$-inch or 1-inch grid paper. Your apartment should include a living room, kitchen, bedroom, bathroom and hallway. What scale did you choose? Explain your choice.

   **b)** Give the scaled dimensions of each piece of furniture listed. Place these in your drawing.

   | | |
   |---|---|
   | Dresser: 2' by 4' | Dining table: 8' by 4' |
   | Bed: 6' by 8' | Desk: 4' by 2' |
   | Couch: 6' by 3' | Bookshelf: 1' by 4' |

   **c)** Write an advertisement for your apartment. Include the actual dimensions of the living room, kitchen and bedroom as well the apartment's total square footage.

# Wrap It Up

What does the scale tell you about a scale drawing?
How are ratios used when making a scale drawing?

MATHEMATICALLY
SPEAKING

▶ enlargement

▶ linear dimension

▶ reduction

▶ scale

▶ scale drawing

 **Write About It**

1. Describe the difference between ratios that produce enlargements and ratios that produce reductions. Give an example of each.

2. What do the following scales mean?

   **a)** 4:1

   **b)** $\frac{1}{2}$ cm to 5 meters

   **c)** 1:60

3. Five different types of model train can be purchased. If a real locomotive is 56 feet long, what is the length in inches of the locomotive in each type of train set? Round your answers to the nearest half-inch.

   **a)** HO scale: 1:87

   **b)** N scale: 1:160

   **c)** O scale: 1:48

   **d)** S scale: 1:64

   **e)** Z scale: 1:220

   **f)** Which model train is the smallest? Explain how you can determine this from the ratios.

**4.** The map shows a portion of Grand Canyon National Park.

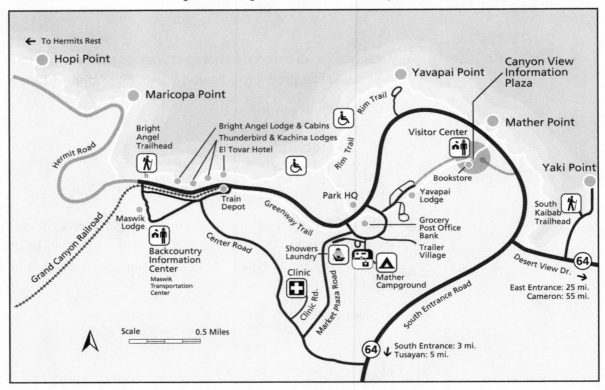

← To Hermits Rest

Hopi Point

Maricopa Point

Yavapai Point

Canyon View Information Plaza

Mather Point

Bright Angel Lodge & Cabins
Thunderbird & Kachina Lodges
El Tovar Hotel

Visitor Center

Bright Angel Trailhead

Rim Trail

Yaki Point

Hermit Road

Rim Trail

Bookstore

Train Depot

Greenway Trail

Park HQ

Yavapai Lodge

South Kaibab Trailhead

Grand Canyon Railroad

Maswik Lodge

Center Road

Grocery
Post Office
Bank

Backcountry Information Center

Showers Laundry

Trailer Village

Desert View Dr. →

64

Maswik Transportation Center

Clinic

Market Plaza Road

Clinic Rd.

Mather Campground

South Entrance Road

East Entrance: 25 mi.
Cameron: 55 mi.

Scale    0.5 Miles

64 ↓ South Entrance: 3 mi.
Tusayan: 5 mi.

**a)** Record the scale for the map as a ratio with and without labels.

**b)** Find the approximate distance along the roads from Bright Angel Trailhead to the Visitor Center.

**c)** Does it make sense to use this map scale for a distance of 200 miles? Why or why not?

**5.** The picture below shows a seventh grade girl, an NBA basketball player and an albatross. The girl has an arm span of 55 inches, the basketball player has an arm span of 83 inches and the albatross has a wingspan of 138 inches. Measure to determine if these pictures were drawn using the same ratio. Explain.

6. Use these scale drawings to determine the actual lengths indicated.

a) Width of human hair, scale of 500:1

b) Gray whale, scale of 1:300

c) Seahorse, scale of 1:4.3

7. Compare the diameter of each circle.

a) What is the value of the ratio of $a:b$?

b) What is the value of the ratio of $b:a$?

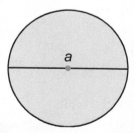

8. Compare the hypotenuses (side length opposite the right angle) of both triangles.

   **a)** What is the value of the ratio of $a:b$?

   **b)** What is the value of the ratio of $b:a$?

   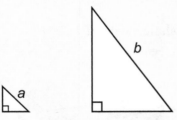

9. Draw a line segment that is 12 centimeters long. Draw other line segments based on the scales given, which compare each segment to the original.

   **a)** $1:3$          **b)** $1.25:1$          **c)** $1:1$

10. Scale drawings of a sports car were made.

   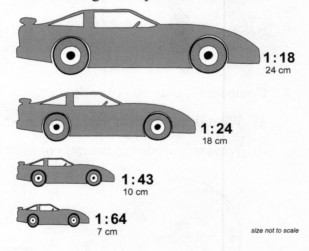

   1:18
   24 cm

   1:24
   18 cm

   1:43
   10 cm

   1:64
   7 cm

   size not to scale

   **a)** Copy and fill in the table.

   | Scale | Length of Sports Car in a Scale Drawing | Length of Real Sports Car |
   |-------|------------------------------------------|----------------------------|
   | 1:18  | 24 cm  |  |
   | 1:24  | 18 cm  |  |
   | 1:43  | 10 cm  |  |
   | 1:64  | 7 cm   |  |

   **b)** Weng Lin stated, "I thought all the scale drawings were of the same sports car, but they can't be." What evidence did Weng Lin use to draw this conclusion?

**c)** Assuming that the data in the table above for the scale of 1 to 18 is accurate, correct the table.

11. Set designers use scale models to plan the scenery for plays. One theater has a rectangular stage that is 64 feet wide and 48 feet deep. A car that is 6.5 feet by 10 feet needs to be onstage. Determine a scale that lets you draw the stage and car on an $8\frac{1}{2}$-by-11-inch piece of paper. Explain your steps and thinking.

**Think Beyond**

12. Measure the dimensions of your bedroom and the length and width of four pieces of furniture. Make a scale drawing of your room and place the four pieces of furniture in the drawing. Give the scale you used.

**Think Back**

13. Which improper fraction is halfway between $-3$ and $-4$?

    **A.** $-\frac{14}{4}$  　　**C.** $-\frac{4}{3}$

    **B.** $-\frac{28}{5}$  　　**D.** $-\frac{7}{3}$

14. Find three pairs of values for $w$ and $h$ that make this inequality true: $\frac{1}{2} + w \leq h$. One of your pairs must include fractions.

15. Which has a greater area, a square with a side length of $4\frac{1}{4}$ meters or a circle with a diameter of $4\frac{1}{4}$ meters? How much greater? You may use a calculator. Round answers to the nearest hundredth of a meter.

16. Annabelle has to decide which of these fractions is greater: $-\frac{3}{5}$ or $-\frac{2}{3}$. She decides that, since $\frac{2}{3} > \frac{3}{5}$, it must also be true that $-\frac{2}{3} > -\frac{3}{5}$. Do you agree or disagree with Annabelle? Explain.

17. Find the explicit rule for this input/output table if the pattern continues as shown.

    | Input | Output |
    |-------|--------|
    | −2 | −8 |
    | −1 | −6 |
    | 0 | −4 |
    | 1 | −2 |
    | 2 | 0 |
    | 3 | 2 |
    | 4 | 4 |

# Enlargements and Reductions

## Start It Off

1. Describe the method you use to write a decimal value as a percent.

2. Why does your method work?

3. Use your method to write the following decimals as percents.

   **a)** 0.08          **d)** 0.005

   **b)** 0.93          **e)** 0.425

   **c)** 0.015         **f)** $0.\overline{3}$

4. How do you write percents for decimals written to thousandths (0.002) or ten-thousandths (0.4567)?

Have you ever enlarged or reduced a picture or photograph? The mathematics behind enlargements and reductions involves ratios.

# Scale Factors

One of these photographs is a correct enlargement of the photograph above. Which one is it?

A                     B                     C

1. a) Measure the lengths, widths and diagonals of the original photograph and the photos labeled A, B and C. Compare the dimensions of the original to the same dimensions in A, B and C. What do you notice?

   b) Which picture was enlarged so that all dimensions have the same scale factor?

The enlarged photograph is 2 times as long and 2 times as wide as the original. The diagonal also is twice as long. The enlargement was created using a scale of 2 to 1. The scale factor is the value of the ratio, which in this case is 2.

When you multiply each of the linear dimensions in an original drawing by a scale factor greater than 1, you get the new dimensions of an enlargement. Sometimes a scale drawing is called an image of the original. The scale factor indicates how many times longer the length, width and diagonal of the image are than the corresponding original dimensions.

2. a) Measure the lengths, widths and diagonals of the original photograph and the reduction above. Write ratios that compare the measures in the reduction to the corresponding measures in the original photograph.

   b) Write the scale factor for this reduction as a fraction and as a decimal.

   c) How many times the length of each dimension of the original drawing is the length of each dimension of the reduction?

How are scales and scale factors related?

Using the reduction of the puppies photograph, the scale is found by comparing the image to the original.

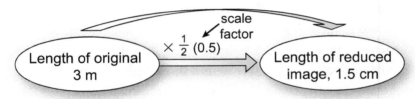

| Length of reduced image (in cm) | 1.5 | 1 | |
|---|---|---|---|
| Length of original drawing (in cm) | 3 | 2 | The scale is 1:2 |

The scale factor is the value of the scale. You multiply the original lengths by the scale factor to determine the lengths of the reduced image.

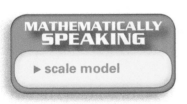

Length of original 3 m  × $\frac{1}{2}$ (0.5) scale factor → Length of reduced image, 1.5 cm

The scale factor is the value of the ratio that compares the image to the original. A scale factor is a multiplication factor.

To determine the dimensions of an enlargement or a reduction, multiply the length and width of the original object by the scale factor.

3. **a)** Why must all the dimensions of the original photograph be multiplied by the same scale factor in order for its image to "look right"?

   **b)** If the scale factor is 1, what will the image of the photograph look like?

   **c)** If the scale factor is $0.\overline{3}$, what will the image look like?

   **d)** If the scale factor for length is 1 and the scale factor for width is $0.\overline{3}$, what will the image look like?

**MATHEMATICALLY SPEAKING**

▶ scale model

**Scale models** are three-dimensional enlargements or reductions of real objects.

**4. a)** The width of the mouth of an average woman is $2\frac{1}{4}$ inches. The width of the mouth of the Statue of Liberty is 3 feet. Assuming that the Statue of Liberty is a scale model of an average woman, what scale factor was used to make the statue?

**b)** The right arm of the Statue of Liberty is 42 feet long. Using the scale factor you found in Part a, how long is the right arm of an average woman? Give your answer in feet and inches.

**c)** The height of a Lilliputian, one of the tiny people in Jonathan Swift's *Gulliver's Travels*, is $5\frac{3}{4}$ inches. What is the height of the real man that the Lilliputian was based upon if the scale factor used was 0.08?

**5.** Write multiplicative sentences that compare the scale models to the original objects for Questions 4a, 4b and 4c.

# Creating an Enlargement

One method for making an enlargement uses a grid. Take a picture such as a smiley face and lightly draw a grid of small squares over it. Pick a scale factor, such as 1.5. Draw a larger grid in which each small square is 1.5 times as long and as wide as the squares on the original grid.

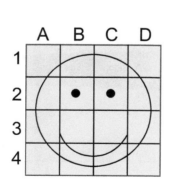

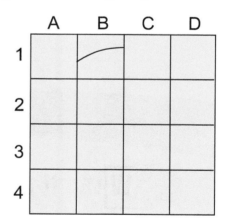

Number the rows 1–4, and label the columns A–D. In each cell in the larger grid, draw the part of the smiley face in the corresponding cell of the smaller grid. Examine cell 1B to see how to get started.

Enlarged or reduced characters are often seen in movies and television. For example, in *Bee Movie*, the size of a real bee was enlarged using a scale factor of 4 so that the bee character was easier to see when flying around humans!

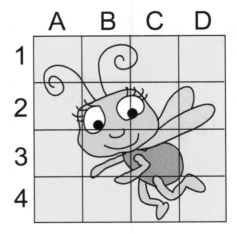

6. Work with a partner to draw an enlargement of the picture of the bug above.

   **a)** Pick a scale factor. Explain what your scale factor means.

   **b)** Draw the enlarged grid. You may need to tape sheets of grid paper together. What are the dimensions of the enlarged grid?

   **c)** In each square in the enlarged grid, draw the part of the bug in the corresponding square of the original grid. Add color and shading to your drawing.

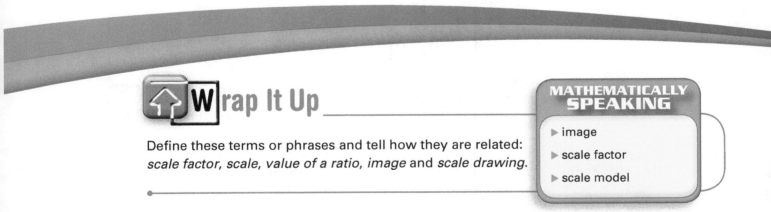

## ⬆W rap It Up _____

Define these terms or phrases and tell how they are related: *scale factor, scale, value of a ratio, image* and *scale drawing.*

**MATHEMATICALLY SPEAKING**

▶ image

▶ scale factor

▶ scale model

**Write About It**

1. Kerilynn wants to make a reduced drawing of an 18" × 24" poster. Pick a scale factor that could be used to draw a reduction of this poster on a regular $8\frac{1}{2}$" × 11" piece of paper. Explain how you determined the scale factor and how you would use it to make the reduced image.

2. In *Bee Movie*, the scale factor used to enlarge the bee was 4. The head of a real bee is $\frac{1}{4}$ inch long and its body is $\frac{3}{8}$ inch long. What was the total length of the enlarged bee in the movie?

3. Fill in the blanks.

   a) The term *factor* is associated with the operation of _____.

   b) When you enlarge a figure, the scale factor is _____.

   c) When you reduce a figure, the scale factor is _____.

4. Give an example of when you would want to view an enlargement of an object. Explain why it would be useful. Then give an example of when you would want to view a reduction and explain why it would be useful.

5. Below is a picture of an ant.

   a) What does a scale factor of 10 mean?

   b) What is the length of the body and head of the actual ant? Show your calculations.

Scale factor of 10

6. Four drawings are enlarged. Measurements from the original drawings and the enlargements are given in the table below.

| | Width of Original (in cm) | Width of Enlargement (in cm) |
|---|---|---|
| Drawing A | 8.3 | 33.2 |
| Drawing B | 2 | 10 |
| Drawing C | 16 | 64 |
| Drawing D | 3.5 | 8.75 |

a) Which drawings have the same scale factor?

b) Are the other drawings enlarged more or less than the drawings in Part a? Explain how you know.

7. Enlarged and reduced copies of this antique baseball ticket can be made using a copy machine. Copy machines list the scale factor as a percent.

a) The image setting on the copy machine is 175%. Write the scale factor as a decimal.

b) If you enlarge the ticket shown by 175%, give the dimensions of the enlarged image.

c) Winston changed the image setting and made a copy of the ticket that was $1\frac{1}{2}$ inches long and $1\frac{1}{8}$ inches tall. What scale factor did he use?

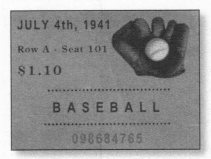

8. a) What does a scale factor of $0.\overline{6}$ mean?

b) Write this scale factor as a fraction.

c) Use the scale factor to draw the image of a 3-inch by 3-inch square.

9. Four drawings are reduced. Measurements from the original drawings and the reductions are given in the table below.

|  | Width of Original (in cm) | Width of Reduction (in cm) |
|---|---|---|
| Drawing E | 2 | $\frac{1}{3}$ |
| Drawing F | 140 | 14 |
| Drawing G | 5 | 1 |
| Drawing H | 72 | 12 |

a) Which drawings have the same scale factor?

b) Are the other drawings reduced more or less than the two drawings in Part a? Explain how you know.

10. In the movie *Honey, I Blew Up the Kid*, a baby that is originally 30 inches tall grows to 7 feet! Later, the baby reaches 50 feet in height.

a) What is the scale factor between the baby's original height and the height of 7 feet?

b) What scale factor was used to enlarge the baby to a height of 50 feet?

11. A scale factor tells us how many times longer or shorter to make each linear measurement in a scale drawing or model. If you wanted to make a scale model of a pencil, list at least three linear measurements that you would need to collect.

12. Indicate the scale (ratio) that was used to make each drawing or model.

a) The handle of a giant spoon is 25 times as long as a handle on a regular spoon.

b) The model of a car has a scale factor of $\frac{1}{84}$.

c) The height of the scale drawing is $\frac{3}{5}$ of the height of the original.

d) An enlarged photograph is 3.5 times as wide as the original photo.

**Think Beyond**

13. Make an enlargement of this cartoon or another cartoon of your choice. Decide on the scale factor. How are the dimensions of the enlargement related to the dimensions of the original cartoon?

**Think Back**

14. True or False?

$$a \cdot \frac{1}{b} = a \div b$$

15. Evaluate these expressions.

   **a)** $|0|$

   **b)** $-|-107|$

   **c)** $\left|-\frac{1}{2}\right|$

   **d)** $-(-|-0.\overline{6}|)$

16. This question was on a quiz Leo took.

   A triangular garden has a base of 12 feet and a height of 20 feet 8 inches. Each square foot can sustain two tomato plants. What is the greatest number of tomato plants that can be planted in this garden?

   Leo showed this work. Identify and correct Leo's mistake.

   $$A = \frac{1}{2}bh$$
   $$= \frac{1}{2}(12)(20.8)$$
   $$= (6)(20.8)$$
   $$= 124.8 \text{ ft.}^2$$

   $124.8 \cdot 2 = 249.6$. At most, 249 tomatoes can be planted in this garden.

17. Mrs. Travon enters a grocery store with $20. She wants to buy boneless swordfish steaks that are $5.99 a pound. First, estimate the number of whole pounds of swordfish she can buy. Next, determine to the nearest hundredth the number of pounds of swordfish Mrs. Travon can buy. Do not use a calculator.

18. **a)** Plot the following points on a coordinate grid: $(-2, 7)$, $(0, 1)$, $(1, -2)$, $(3, -8)$.

   **b)** Draw a line through the points. Give three more points in Quadrant II that will be on the line.

   **c)** List three more points in Quadrant IV that will be on the line.

# Similar Polygons

→ **Start It Off**

How do you change a fraction to a percent? Some students write fractions first as decimals and then as percents. Other students write fractions as equivalent fractions with denominators of 100 and then write these as percents.

1. Describe a method for writing a fraction whose decimal equivalent terminates, such as $\frac{11}{20}$, as a percent. Show how your method works with this fraction.

2. Describe a method for writing a fraction whose decimal equivalent repeats, such as $\frac{1}{7}$, as a percent. Show how your method works with this fraction.

3. Write these fractions as percents.

   a) $\frac{14}{25}$                    d) $\frac{3}{20}$

   b) $\frac{2}{3}$                     e) $\frac{1}{9}$

   c) $\frac{5}{6}$

**MATHEMATICALLY SPEAKING**

▸ similar

Similar is an important word in mathematics. Similar figures are defined informally as being the same shape but different sizes. In this lesson you will explore the characteristics of similar polygons and develop a precise definition of similarity.

**1.** What is the everyday meaning of the word *similar*?

When you enlarged or reduced drawings using scale factors in the last lesson, you were making similar figures. We will use these ideas to help you understand the mathematical meaning of similar polygons.

# Congruent or Similar?

**MATHEMATICALLY SPEAKING**

▸ congruent
▸ symbol "≅"

When two polygons are congruent, they are exactly the same shape and size. For example, $\triangle ABC$ is congruent to $\triangle DEF$. The angles in both triangles are identical. The side lengths in both triangles are identical. The symbol for "is congruent to" is ≅.

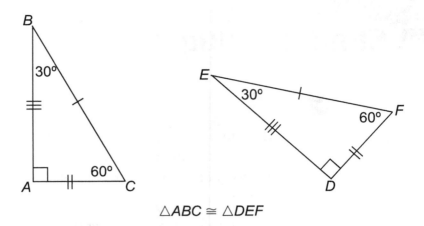

$\triangle ABC \cong \triangle DEF$

2.  **a)** If you start with two congruent figures and flip or turn one of them, will the figures still be congruent? Why or why not?

    **b)** Why don't mathematicians just say that two shapes are equal?

    **c)** How are the symbols for "is congruent to" and "is equal to" alike? How are they different?

    **d)** What scale factor is used to create a congruent figure?

It is easier to describe congruent and similar figures if the figures are named. Polygons are named by listing the vertices in order, moving usually in a counterclockwise direction. You can start at any vertex. For example, *FORK* is one possible name for the square below.

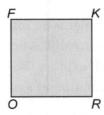

3.  Name the following polygons.

    **a)** 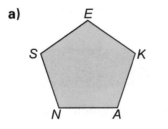  **b)** 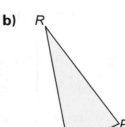  **c)**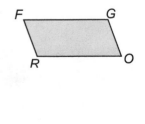

    **d)** Is the triangle in Part b congruent to $\triangle DEF$ or $\triangle ABC$ above? Why or why not?

# What's the Angle?

**MATHEMATICALLY SPEAKING**

▶ corresponding angles

When two shapes are similar then corresponding angles are congruent. Corresponding angles are angles that have the same position relative to the other angles in two related polygons.

## Example

Which angles are corresponding angles in the similar hexagons below? How can you check if they are congruent?

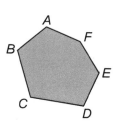 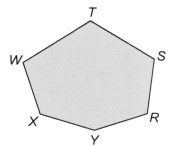

- Turn or flip the shapes in your mind so they have the same orientation. How would you turn hexagon *RSTWXY* so it is oriented like hexagon *ABCDEF*?

- Use tracing paper to copy hexagon ABCDEF. Then check whether angles in *ABCDEF* are congruent to the corresponding angles in hexagon *RSTWXY*.

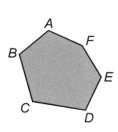 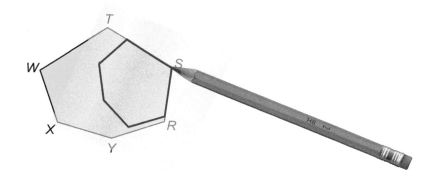

- Use a protractor to check which angles are congruent.

The corresponding angles are:

| | | |
|---|---|---|
| $\angle A \cong \angle R$ | $\angle B \cong \angle S$ | $\angle C \cong \angle T$ |
| $\angle D \cong \angle W$ | $\angle E \cong \angle X$ | $\angle F \cong \angle Y$ |

Two polygons may be similar if all pairs of corresponding angles are congruent.

**4. a)** Measure the angles in polygons *ABCDEF* and *RSTWXY* in the example above.

**b)** Compare the angles in the hexagons in the Example to the angles in hexagon *GHIJKL* below. Is ∠*G* congruent to ∠*A*? Is ∠*K* congruent to ∠*X*?

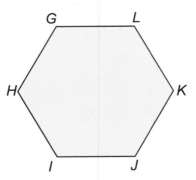

**5. a)** Measure the angles in the following shapes. List the shapes in which all the corresponding angles are congruent.

**b)** Examine the shapes with congruent angles. Do you think these shapes are similar? Why or why not?

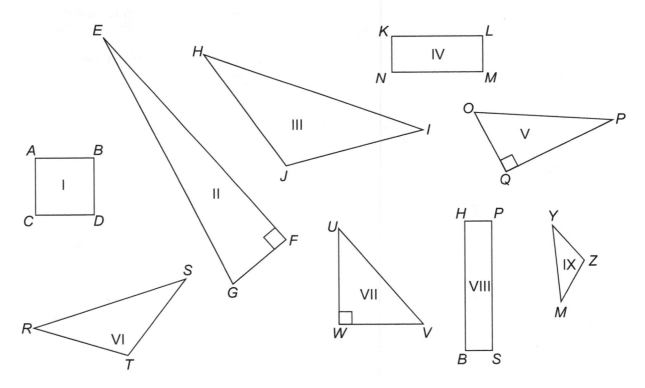

## MATHEMATICALLY SPEAKING

▶ corresponding sides

Corresponding angles must be congruent for two polygons to be similar, but angles are not the only thing to consider. Similar polygons are related in other ways that have to do with ratios of the lengths of corresponding sides. Corresponding sides are sides that have the same position relative to the other sides in two related polygons. Look carefully at the figures below to help you figure out the ratio connection.

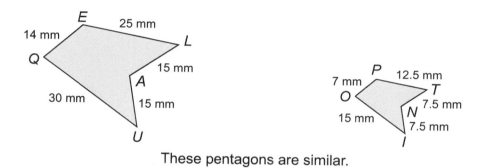

These pentagons are similar.

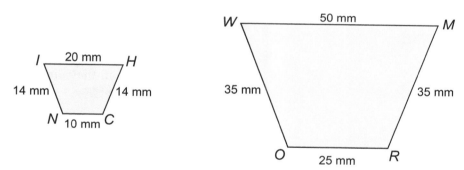

These trapezoids are similar.

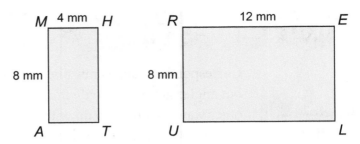

These rectangles are *not* similar.

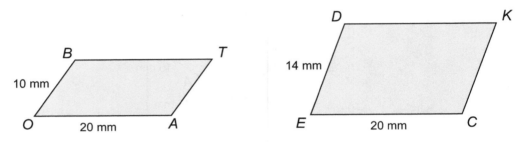

These parallelograms are *not* similar.

**6.** **a)** Study the figures. Look for relationships between the lengths of corresponding sides of the similar figures. Describe what makes two polygons similar.

**b)** Tony said, "Just because two shapes have corresponding congruent angles, it doesn't mean they are similar." Do you agree or disagree with Tony? Explain.

**7.** **a)** Form ratios that compare each side length in *EQUAL* to the corresponding side length in *POINT*. Are these ratios equal?

**b)** Give the scale factor if *EQUAL* is the original shape and *POINT* is the image.

**c)** Give the scale factor if *POINT* is the original shape and *EQUAL* is the image.

MATHEMATICALLY
SPEAKING

▸ symbol "∼"

When two polygons are similar, the ratios formed by corresponding sides are all equal. The symbol for "is similar to" is ∼ .

| SYMBOL | MEANING |
|---|---|
| ∼ | is similar to |
| *EQUAL* ∼ *POINT* | Pentagon *EQUAL* is similar to pentagon *POINT*. |

**8.** Form ratios that compare corresponding sides of trapezoids *WORM* and *INCH*. What is the value of the four ratios?

9. **a)** List the corresponding sides of rectangles *MATH* and *RULE*.

   **b)** Form ratios that compare each side length of *MATH* to the corresponding side length of *RULE*. Are these ratios equal?

   **c)** Why aren't these rectangles similar?

10. Write a mathematical definition for *similar polygons* that includes corresponding angles and corresponding sides. Explain your definition.

# Using Similarity

When two polygons are similar, you can find missing side lengths by forming equivalent ratios that compare the lengths of corresponding sides and then solving the proportion.

Note that the notation $ADCB \sim WZYX$ not only tells you that the rectangles are similar but also indicates which angles correspond to each other. $\angle A$ corresponds to $\angle W$ since they both are listed first; $\angle D$ corresponds to $\angle Z$ since they both are listed second; and so on.

### Example

$ADCB \sim WZYX$. Find the length of $\overline{ZY}$.

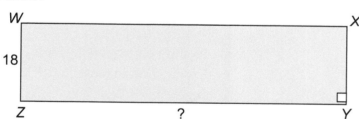

To find the length of $\overline{ZY}$, compare corresponding side lengths. Side $\overline{AD}$ corresponds to $\overline{WZ}$. $\overline{DC}$ corresponds to $\overline{ZY}$. Since the ratios of the lengths of corresponding sides in similar figures are equal, we write:

$$\frac{AD}{WZ} = \frac{DC}{ZY}$$

Each ratio in the proportion compares a side length in one rectangle to the corresponding side length in the other rectangle. That is, the proportion compares side lengths *between* the two rectangles.

$$\frac{6}{18} = \frac{24}{ZY}$$

Solve the proportion.

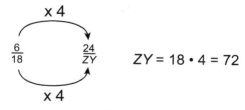

$ZY = 18 \cdot 4 = 72$

The length of $\overline{ZY}$ is 72 units.

**11. a)** Rectangle *ADCB* in the example is a reduction of rectangle *WZYX*. What scale factor was used in this reduction?

**b)** You can also state that *WZYX* is an enlargement of *ADCB*. What scale factor was used to create the enlargement?

**c)** How are the ratios in Parts a and b related? Is this always the case?

---

 **Let's Review**     The sum of the measures of the angles in a triangle is 180°.

---

**12.** △*SUB* ~ △*DIV*

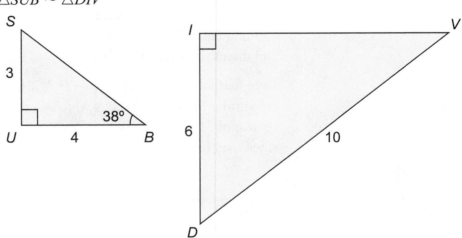

**a)** Identify corresponding sides and angles between the two triangles. Explain how to move △*DIV* to make it easier to identify corresponding angles and sides

**b)** Determine the measures of ∠*D* and ∠*V*.

**c)** Find the lengths of $\overline{SB}$ and $\overline{IV}$.

When two polygons are similar, the ratios that compare corresponding side lengths are equal. The proportion shows the connection *between* the two polygons. You can also form ratios that compare side lengths *within* each polygon.

Caroline wrote a ratio to compare two side lengths in △*SUB*. She then set this ratio equal to the ratio of the two corresponding side lengths in △*DIV*. Her proportion compares side lengths *within* △*SUB* to side lengths *within* △*DIV*. Sometimes proportions based on ratios within similar polygons are easier to solve.

$$\frac{SU}{UB} = \frac{DI}{IV}$$

$$\overset{\times 2}{\frac{3}{4} = \frac{6}{IV}}$$

$$IV = 8$$

# Wrap It Up

In this lesson, you investigated what it means for two polygons to be similar and learned about setting up proportions using *between* and *within* ratios.

Explain what the phrases *between* ratios and *within* ratios mean when setting up proportions involving similar figures. Give an example. Why are both types useful for identifying missing values?

▸ congruent

▸ corresponding angles

▸ corresponding sides

▸ similar

▸ symbol "≅"

▸ symbol "∼"

## On Your Own

**Write About It**

1. How are congruent figures and similar figures the same and how are they different?

2. Robin stated, "Two polygons that are similar are never congruent." Explain why you agree or disagree.

3. The following shapes have corresponding sides that form equivalent ratios. Are the shapes similar? Why or why not?

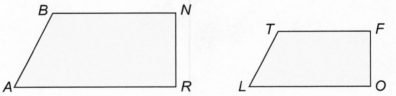

4. **a)** List the corresponding sides and angles for these two trapezoids.

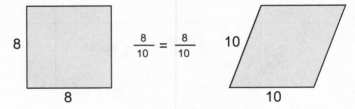

   **b)** Are these trapezoids similar?

   **c)** How do you know?

5. Are these parallelograms similar? Explain why or why not.

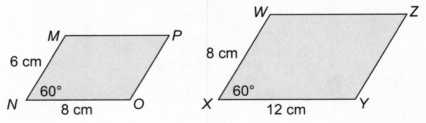

Use the following three triangles for Questions 6–9.

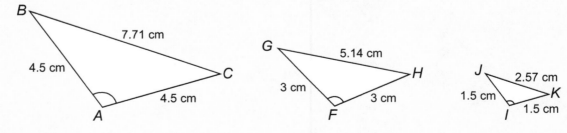

**6.** Form ratios that compare the lengths of corresponding sides of the following triangles. Measure in centimeters to the nearest tenth. Find the value of the ratios.

    **a)** △ABC and △FGH    **b)** △ABC and △IJK    **c)** △FGH and △IJK

**7.** What are the measures of the angles in each triangle?

**8. a)** What is the scale factor between △ABC and △FGH?

    **b)** Between △ABC and △IJK?

    **c)** Between △FGH and △IJK?

**9.** Are these three triangles similar? Explain why or why not.

**10.** Jake wrote, "Two polygons that are congruent are always similar." Explain why you agree or disagree.

**11.** △FIT ~ △REC

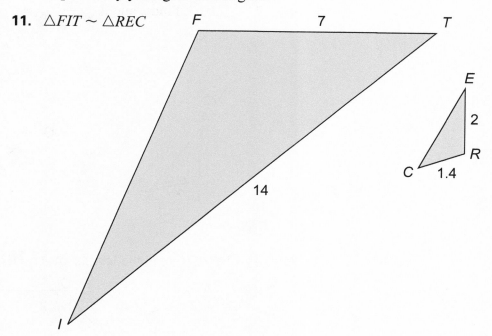

    **a)** Marcus has been absent. Explain to him how to identify the corresponding sides of these similar triangles.

    **b)** Use *within* ratios to write a proportion to find the length of $\overline{EC}$. Use *between* ratios to write a different proportion to find the length of $\overline{EC}$.

    **c)** Which proportions from Part b are the easiest to solve using mental math?

    **d)** Find the length of $\overline{FI}$.

    **e)** What scale factors describe the relationship between the two triangles?

**12.** *SMAL ~ BIGE*. Find *x* and *y*.

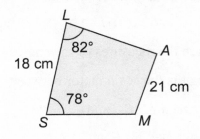 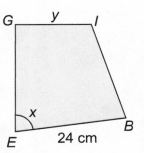

For Questions 13–17, use the definition of *similar polygons*. All measurements are in centimeters. Some drawings are not to scale.

**13.** △*ACE ~* △*DOG*. Find *x* and *y*.

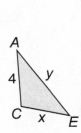 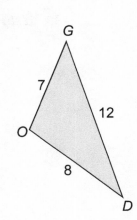

**14.** *PINTA ~ HORSE*. Find the lengths of $\overline{AT}$, $\overline{HO}$, $\overline{OR}$ and $\overline{EH}$.

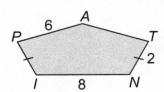 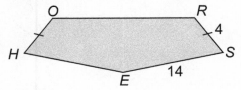

**15.** *PICK ~ MATH*. Find the lengths of $\overline{PI}$, $\overline{IC}$, $\overline{TH}$, $\overline{MH}$ and $\overline{MA}$.

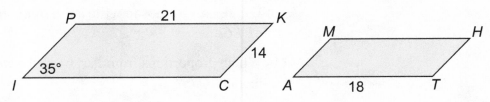

**16.** *ROITA ~ MELDU*

**a)** $\overline{RA}$ = _____

**c)** $\overline{LE}$ = _____

**b)** $\overline{TI}$ = _____

**d)** $\overline{UD}$ = _____

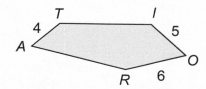

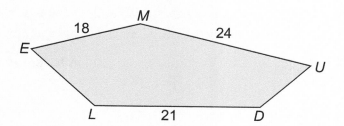

**17.** Pedro noticed that depending on how he set up the ratios in Question 16, some calculations were easier than others. He used both *between* ratios and *within* ratios to write his proportions. Give an example of each type. Explain how these proportions are different.

**18.** *RAIN ~ STOP*

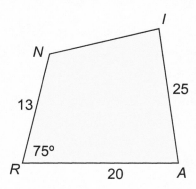

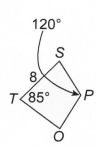

**a)** $\overline{SP}$ = _____

**b)** $m\angle A$ = _____

**c)** $m\angle N$ = _____

**d)** $\overline{TO}$ = _____

**e)** $m\angle I$ = _____

**19. a)** Draw two similar parallelograms. Make sure corresponding angles are congruent! Give side lengths.

**b)** Write a proportion that compares corresponding sides.

**c)** Simplify the ratios in the proportion. What is the scale factor between shapes?

**20.** One definition of *similarity* states, "Similar figures have corresponding sides that are in proportion and corresponding angles that are congruent." What does the phrase "corresponding sides that are in proportion" mean?

 **Think Beyond**

**21.** Ryan thinks that all circles are similar to each other. Do you agree or disagree with Ryan? Explain.

**Think Back**

**22.** Write each percent as a decimal and a simplified fraction.

**a)** 91%

**b)** 2.5%

**c)** 15%

**23.** Find the perimeter of a rectangular garden whose longer side is $18\frac{2}{9}$ feet long and whose shorter side is half the length of the long side.

**24.** Active Life, a sport supply store, is going out of business. You purchase three T-shirts that are marked 20% off their regular price of $12.50. What is the sale price of the three T-shirts all together?

**25.** Whitman showed his work to solve $-3x + 5 = 18$. Find and correct his mistake.

$$-3x + 5 = 18$$
$$-3x = 18$$
$$x = -6 + -5$$
$$x = -11$$

**26.** List three facts about absolute value.

# Ratios and Slope

→ **Start It Off**

1. Where have you heard the word *slope* before? What does it mean?

2. For what objects is their steepness or slope important? Think about real-world situations.

3. The mathematical meaning of *slope* involves the steepness of a line. Draw a horizontal line segment. Using this segment as a base, draw two steep lines extending from the base. Label them *line 1* and *line 2*.

4. Now draw two more lines that are not as steep as the first two. The slopes of these lines are less than the slopes of the lines in Question 3.

5. Describe in words the steepness of a horizontal line.

Let's use what you have learned about similarity and ratios to help you understand slope. Examine the rectangles below.

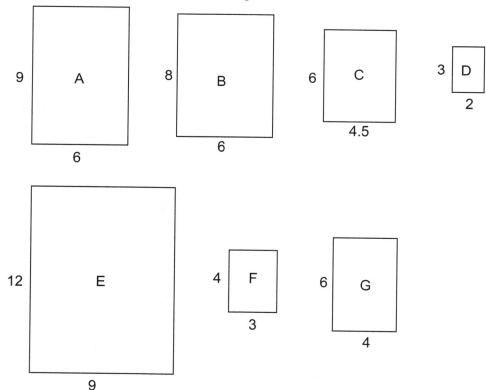

1. **a)** Sort the rectangles into two groups so that the rectangles in each group are similar.

   **b)** Explain why the rectangles in each group are similar.

Draw Quadrant I of a coordinate plane on grid paper. Draw similar rectangles A, D and G on the grid. Place the rectangles with one vertex at the origin and the shorter side along the *x*-axis.

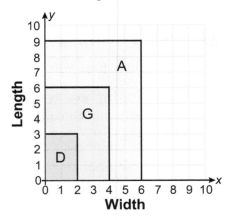

2. **a)** Pick a scale factor less than 1. Using this scale factor, determine the dimensions of a new rectangle that is similar to D. Add it to your graph and label it H.

   **b)** Give the dimensions of another similar rectangle. Add it to your graph and label it I.

3. Write a ratio that compares the length (*y*-value) to the width (*x*-value) for each rectangle on the grid. Find the value of each ratio. What do you notice?

4. **a)** Draw the diagonal from the origin to the opposite vertex of each rectangle. Use the coordinates of points on this line to complete the table.

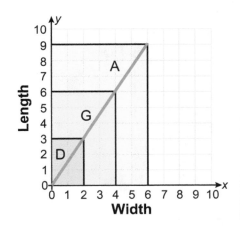

| x | y |
|---|---|
| 0 | 0 |
| 1 | |
| 2 | |
| 3 | |
| 4 | |
| 5 | |
| 6 | |

   **b)** Are the pairs of *x*- and *y*-values in the table related to the dimensions of the rectangles? Explain.

   **c)** Determine the equation of the line that relates the *x*- and *y*-values.

The explicit rule that relates the *x*-values and *y*-values in this table is also the equation of this line. Notice that the value of the ratio that compares the lengths to the widths within each rectangle is part of the equation. This is the slope of the diagonal line and indicates its steepness. The slope of a straight line is always the value of a ratio. This ratio is the change in the vertical distance to the change in the horizontal distance between points on the line. In this case it is length to width ratio of the rectangles.

5. **a)** What is the slope of the line in Question 4?

   **b)** Is the slope of the line the same along the whole line? Why or why not?

   **c)** Why do the diagonals of the rectangles form a straight line?

6. **a)** Examine the other group of similar rectangles (B, C, E and F). Explain why they are similar.

   **b)** Draw a coordinate grid and trace the rectangles so one vertex is at (0, 0) and the longer side is along the *x*-axis. Draw the diagonal from the origin through the opposite vertex of each rectangle. Create a table to relate the *x*- and *y*-values.

   **c)** Determine the equation of the line. How are the slope of the line and the value of the ratio that compares *y*-values to *x*-values related?

   **d)** Draw a second coordinate grid and place the rectangles so that the short sides are along the *x*-axis. Draw the diagonal from the origin through the opposite vertex of each rectangle. Create a table that relates the *y*- and *x*-values. Determine the equation of the line.

   **e)** What is the slope of this new diagonal line? How does changing the placement of the rectangles on the grid affect the steepness of the diagonal line and the ratio of *y*-values to *x*-values?

 **W**rap It Up

How are the ratios of length to width of similar rectangles and slopes of their diagonals connected? Use examples from this lesson to explain.

**Write
About It**

1. The lines you drew in this lesson all represent proportional relationships. How are the equation of a proportional relationship and the slope of the line it describes related? Why?

2. Copy the graph below. Add three rectangles, each with a vertex at the origin and the opposite vertex on the graphed line. What is the slope of the line?

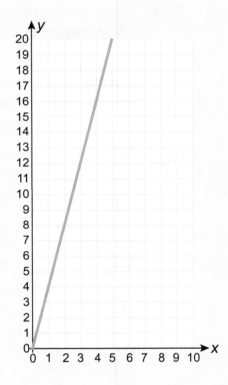

For Questions 3–5:

a) Shape A is the original shape. Determine the scale factor that produces Shape B.

b) Shape B is the original shape. Determine the scale factor that produces Shape A.

**3.**

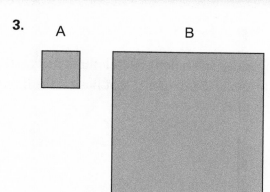

A           B

**4.**

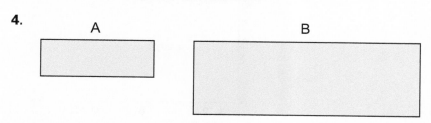

A           B

**5.**

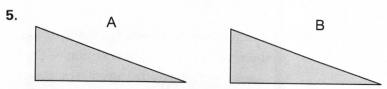

A           B

**6. a)** If the squares in Question 3 were placed on a coordinate grid, what slope would describe their diagonals?

 **Hint**
See page 167

**b)** If the rectangles in Question 4 were placed on a coordinate grid, what slope would describe their diagonals?

 **Hint**
See page 167

**7.** Give a $y:x$ ratio for each of the following slopes of lines that pass through the origin:

**a)** slope $= 5$

**b)** slope $= \frac{2}{3}$

**c)** slope $= \frac{7}{10}$

**d)** slope $= 2$

8. Copy the graph below. Sketch three rectangles that have one vertex at the origin and a diagonal that lies on the line graphed. What is the slope of the line?

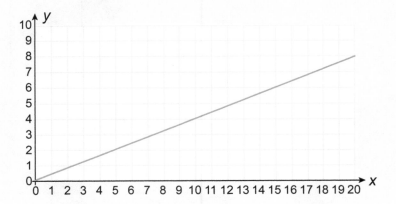

9. For each table, determine the value of the ratio that relates the y-values to the x-values. Write the equation of the line.

a)

| x | y |
|---|---|
| 0 | 0 |
| 1 | 7 |
| 2 | 14 |
| 3 | 21 |
| 4 | 28 |
| 5 | 35 |

b)

| x | y |
|---|---|
| 0 | 0 |
| 1 | 0.89 |
| 2 | 1.78 |
| 3 | 2.67 |
| 4 | 3.56 |

c)

| x | y |
|---|---|
| 0 | 0 |
| 2 | 30 |
| 3 | 45 |
| 5 | 75 |
| 10 | 150 |

Use the graph to answer Questions 10–14.

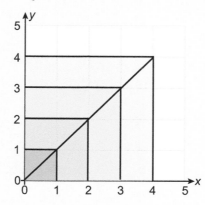

10. Using the largest square on the grid as the original figure, what scale factors could be used to produce the three smaller squares?

11. What $y : x$ ratio describes this set of squares? Record this ratio in simplified form. What is the value of the ratio?

12. Use the diagonal from the origin through the opposite vertex of the squares to create a table that relates the $x$- and $y$-values. Determine the equation of this line.

13. How are the slope of the line and the ratio between the $y$- and $x$-values related?

14. Without plotting the point, will (17, 17) be on this line? How do you know?

15. Tutita stated, "All squares are similar to each other. I can always find a scale factor that relates one to another." Do you agree or disagree with Tutita? Give at least three examples to support your position.

16. Give the dimensions of a group of three rectangles that have the same length-to-width ratio. Sketch the rectangles on a coordinate grid. What slope describes the line that includes their diagonals?

17. For each equation, list the slope and give the dimensions of three rectangles whose diagonals would lie on the line.

   a) $y = 3x$

   b) $y = \frac{2}{3}x$

   c) $y = \frac{4}{5}x$

   d) $y = 2x$

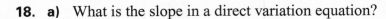

**18. a)** What is the slope in a direct variation equation?

   **b)** What ratio is used to determine slope?

   **c)** Explain how slope and proportional relationships are related.

**19. a)** What is the slope of each of the following lines?

$$y = -\frac{1}{2}x \qquad y = -4x \qquad y = -\frac{3}{4}x$$

   **b)** Write a ratio that describes the slope of each line.

   **c)** Describe how these lines will look on the coordinate plane. How is this reflected in the slope?

**20.** Ray had to answer this question on last night's homework.

*Evaluate* $\frac{1}{4}(6x + 24)$.

Ray said the answer was $-11\frac{1}{2}$. Is he right? If he is right, show the work to verify. If Ray is wrong, correct his mistake.

**21.** Estimate the quotient, and then find the exact quotient. Do not use a calculator.

$$-87.978 \div -8.6$$

**22.** The heights of the five starters on a basketball team are $63\frac{1}{2}$ inches, $66\frac{1}{4}$ inches, 69 inches, $62\frac{5}{8}$ inches and $72\frac{1}{4}$ inches. Find the mean height of the team.

**23.** If one sheet of aluminum is 0.045 inch thick, find the total thickness of a stack of 75 sheets.

**24.** Which of the following represent rational numbers?

   **a)** 5

   **b)** $\frac{0}{8}$

   **c)** $12 \div 0$

   **d)** $2\frac{1}{5}$

   **e)** 8.09

   **f)** $\sqrt{6}$

# Perimeters and Areas of Similar Polygons

➡️ **Start It Off**

1. Write the following percents as decimals.

   **a)** 58%  **d)** 100%

   **b)** 1%  **e)** 29.5%

   **c)** 83.25%

2. Write the following percents as fractions in simplified form.

   **a)** 58%  **d)** 36%

   **b)** 12.5%  **e)** 60%

   **c)** $33.\overline{3}$%

3. **a)** List three percents whose simplified fraction forms have a denominator of 100.

   **b)** List three percents whose simplified fraction forms are unit fractions.

   **c)** List three percents whose simplified fraction forms have a denominator of 8.

Leo and Stephanie are organizing an Earth Day cleanup. Students, parents, teachers and friends will pick up trash in a local park on Saturday morning. Leo and Stephanie decided to send out e-mails about the event and also hang a large poster in the lobby of the school. They want to enlarge the following poster so it has a length of 10 feet.

$1\frac{1}{2}$ ft.

30 in.

1. **a)** What is the area of the original poster?

   **b)** How much paper will Leo and Stephanie need for the enlarged poster?

   **c)** Explain your method for finding the area of the enlarged poster.

You can also determine the area of the enlarged poster using the area of the original shape because the scale factor is related to the area and perimeter of an image.

2.  a)  Explain why the small and large squares shown are similar.

    b)  What scale factor was used to create the enlarged square?

    c)  What is the perimeter and area of the enlarged square?

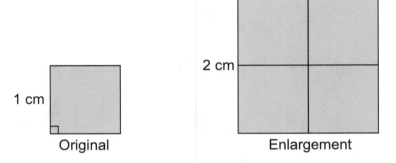

Original

Enlargement

3.  Copy the table below. Pick several sizes of squares and enlarge each using a scale factor of 2. Record the dimensions, perimeter and area of the original square and the enlargement.

| Dimensions (cm) | | Perimeters (cm) | | Areas (cm²) | |
|---|---|---|---|---|---|
| Original | Enlargement: scale factor = 2 | Original | Enlargement: scale factor = 2 | Original | Enlargement: scale factor = 2 |
| 1 × 1 | 2 × 2 | 4 | 8 | 1 | 4 |
| 3 × 3 | 6 × 6 | | | | |
| | | | | | |
| | | | | | |
| | | | | | |
| n × n | | | | | |

4.  a)  Examine the perimeter columns in the table. How many times the perimeters of the originals are the perimeters of the enlargements?

    b)  Why does this pattern occur? Explain using words and symbols.

    c)  Represent the perimeter of a square enlarged by a scale factor of 2 if each side of the original square has a length of $n$.

5. **a)** Examine the area columns in the table. How many times the areas of the originals are the areas of the enlargements?

   **b)** How might the areas of the enlargements be related to the scale factor of 2 and the areas of the originals?

   **c)** Represent the area of a square enlarged by a scale factor of 2 if each side of the original square has a length of *n*.

6. **a)** Start with a 6-cm-by-6-cm square. What is its perimeter and area?

   **b)** Imagine reducing the square using a scale factor of $\frac{1}{2}$. What is the perimeter of the reduction? What is the perimeter of a reduction of the original using a scale factor of $\frac{1}{3}$?

   **c)** What fraction of the perimeter of the $6 \times 6$ square is the perimeter of each reduction?

   **d)** Consider again reducing the $6 \times 6$ square using a scale factor of $\frac{1}{2}$. What is the area of the reduction? What is the area of a reduction of the original with a scale factor of $\frac{1}{3}$?

   **e)** What fraction of the area of the original square is the area of each reduction?

# Enlargements and Reductions of Polygons

Do the patterns you discovered for the perimeter and area of enlarged and reduced squares hold when you enlarge and reduce other shapes?

Mathematicians often use the variable *k* to represent a scale factor. *k* can stand for any number, such as $k = 4$ or $k = \frac{3}{4}$.

original

$k = \frac{3}{4}$

$k = 4$

7.  **a)** Start with a 1 cm × 1 cm square. If $k = 2$, what is the perimeter of the enlarged square? If $k = 3$, what is the perimeter of the enlarged square? If $k = \frac{1}{2}$, what is the perimeter of the reduced square?

    **b)** What effect does the scale factor, $k$, have on the perimeter of scaled squares? Do you think this generalization holds for other shapes? Why or why not?

The original rectangle above is 3 mm × 1 mm. The enlarged rectangle is 12 mm × 4 mm, and the reduced rectangle is $2\frac{1}{4}$ mm × $\frac{3}{4}$ mm. Is the area of the enlargement 4 times the area of the original? Is the area of the reduction $\frac{3}{4}$ times the area of the original?

8.  Stephanie and Leo discussed their methods for finding the areas of the enlargements and reductions of the original rectangle.

*I first find the area of the original rectangle. Then I multiply that area by 16 when the scale factor is 4 and by $\frac{9}{16}$ when the scale factor is $\frac{3}{4}$.*

*I first use the scale factor to find the dimensions of the enlarged or the reduced rectangle. Then I use the new dimensions of the rectangle to find its area.*

    **a)** Do both methods work? Why or why not?

    **b)** Why did Leo multiply the area of the original rectangle by 16 to find the area of the enlargement?

    **c)** Why did Leo multiply the area of the original rectangle by $\frac{9}{16}$ to determine the area of the reduction?

    **d)** Which method has fewer steps? Why is this important to consider?

    **e)** Which method do you prefer?

How is the area of a scaled figure affected by the scale factor, $k$?

*Area of scaled shape = $k^2$ · area of original shape*

**Visual Explanation**

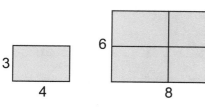 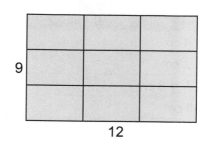 

original

$k = 1$

$A = 12$ cm²

$k = 2$

$A = 4 \cdot 12$ cm²

$= 48$ cm²

$k = 3$

$A = 9 \cdot 12$ cm²

$= 108$ cm²

$k = \frac{1}{2}$

$A = \left(\frac{1}{4}\right) \cdot 12$ cm²

$= 3$ cm²

• The area of the enlargement is four times the area of the original rectangle when $k = 2$.

• The area of the enlargement is nine times the area of the original rectangle when $k = 3$.

• The area of the reduction is $\frac{1}{4}$ times the area of the original rectangle when $k = \frac{1}{2}$.

**Symbolic Explanation**

Original rectangle has dimensions 3 cm by 4 cm, so $A = 12$ cm².

Area of enlargement when $k = 2$

| | |
|---|---|
| $A = (3 \cdot 2) \cdot (4 \cdot 2)$ | Multiply each dimension of the rectangle by 2 since $k = 2$. |
| $= (3 \cdot 4) \cdot (2 \cdot 2)$ | Rearrange the order and grouping of the factors. |
| $= 12 \cdot 4$ | original area times $2^2$ or 4 |
| $= 12 \cdot 2^2$ | original area times $k^2$ when $k = 2$ |
| $= 48$ cm² | |

Area of enlargement when $k = 3$

| | |
|---|---|
| $A = (3 \cdot 3) \cdot (4 \cdot 3)$ | Triple each dimension of the rectangle since $k = 3$. |
| $= (3 \cdot 4) \cdot (3 \cdot 3)$ | Rearrange the order and grouping of the factors. |
| $= 12 \cdot 9$ | original area times 9 |
| $= 12 \cdot 3^2$ | original area times $k^2$ when $k = 3$ |
| $= 108$ cm² | |

Area of reduction when $k = \frac{1}{2}$

| | |
|---|---|
| $A = \left(3 \cdot \frac{1}{2}\right) \cdot \left(4 \cdot \frac{1}{2}\right)$ | Halve each dimension of the rectangle since $k = \frac{1}{2}$. |
| $= (3 \cdot 4) \cdot \left(\frac{1}{2} \cdot \frac{1}{2}\right)$ | Rearrange the order and grouping of the factors. |
| $= 12 \cdot \frac{1}{4}$ | original area times $\frac{1}{4}$ |
| $= 12 \cdot \left(\frac{1}{2}\right)^2$ | original area times $k^2$ when $k = \frac{1}{2}$ |
| $= 3$ cm² | |

9. Use either method to determine the areas of enlarged and reduced shapes. Copy and complete the table.

| | Original Figure | Area of Original (cm²) | Area of Enlargement (cm²) $k = 2$ | Area of Reduction (cm²) $k = \frac{1}{2}$ |
|---|---|---|---|---|
| a) | Rectangle, $l = 2$ cm, $w = 4$ cm | | | |
| b) | Rectangle, $l = 6$ cm, $w = 2$ cm | | | |
| c) | Parallelogram, $b = 9$ cm, $h = 8$ cm | | | |
| d) | Triangle, $b = 4$ cm, $h = 10$ cm | | | |
| e) | Think Beyond Circle, $r = 1$ cm | | | |
| f) | Think Beyond Circle, $r = 4$ cm | | | |

10. a) Explain using visuals why the area of an enlarged rectangle is not four times the area of the original rectangle when $k = 4$.

   b) Explain using symbols why the area of a reduced rectangle is $\frac{1}{9}$ the area of the original rectangle for a scale factor of $\frac{1}{3}$.

11. What properties can be used to explain Step 2?

   Step 1: $A = \left(3 \cdot \frac{1}{2}\right) \cdot \left(4 \cdot \frac{1}{2}\right)$

   Step 2: $A = (3 \cdot 4) \cdot \left(\frac{1}{2} \cdot \frac{1}{2}\right)$

# ⬆W rap It Up

How do the areas of two-dimensional shapes change when they are enlarged by a scale factor of 5 or reduced by a scale factor of $\frac{1}{5}$? Generalize this relationship using the variable $k$ to represent any scale factor.

**Write About It**

1. An enlarged rectangle has an area of 200 square cm. The scale factor used to enlarge this rectangle was 5. What are the possible whole number dimensions of the original rectangle? Explain your reasoning and show all your steps.

2. An enlarged square has an area that is 64 times the area of the original 1 cm × 1 cm square. What scale factor was used?

3. A square has an area of 36 cm². If the square is enlarged using a scale factor of 3, determine the enlarged:

   **a)** side length

   **b)** perimeter

   **c)** area

4. Miniature copies of a painting that is 20 inches by 30 inches are going to be made using different scale factors. For each scale factor, determine the amount of framing that will be needed for the miniature.

   **a)** scale factor $= \frac{1}{4}$

   **b)** scale factor $= 0.1$

   **c)** Find the area of the miniature paintings in Parts a and b.

5. The area of an enlarged square is 144 cm². Determine all possible whole number side lengths for the original square. Find the scale factor that would be used with each original square to create the enlargement.

6. Kayla thinks that when you double both the length and width of a flat screen TV, the overall area is doubled. Do you agree or disagree with Kayla? Why?

7. The size of the rectangular garage on a blueprint is 6 inches by 7 inches. The ratio used to draw the blueprint is $\frac{1}{4}$ inch : 1 foot.

   **a)** What are the dimensions of the actual garage?

   **b)** What is the area of the actual garage?

8. Kenley is tiling a bathroom floor that is 3 m long by 2 m wide. She is using tiny tiles that are each 1 square cm. Kenley says that all she has to do is multiply 6 by 100 to find the number of small tiles. Catherine disagrees and says you have to multiply 6 by 1,000. Who is right? How many tiles will Kenley need?

9. A square has a side length of 12 inches. Using a scale factor of 0.5, what is the area of the image? Use two different methods to solve this problem.

10. Copy and complete the table.

| Original Figure | Scale Factor | Area of Enlargement |
|---|---|---|
| a) Square, $s = 3.5$ cm | 10 | |
| b) Rectangle, 5 cm $\times$ 9 cm | | 180 cm² |
| c) Triangle, $b = 4$ cm, $h = 6$ cm | 1.5 | |
| d) Circle, $r = 3$ cm | 5 | |

11. The infield area between bases on an official major league baseball diamond is 8,100 square feet. The distance between consecutive bases on an official fast-pitch softball diamond is $\frac{2}{3}$ the distance on a major league baseball field. What is the infield area of a fast-pitch softball diamond?

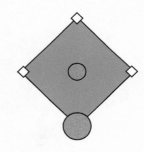

12. a) A sprinkler sprays water in a circle with a diameter of 10 feet. If the diameter is increased to 20 feet, how much more land, in square feet, is watered? Round your answer to the nearest hundredth.

   b) How many times as much area receives water?

13. Copy and complete the table.

| Original Figure | Scale Factor | Area of Reduction |
|---|---|---|
| a) Square, $s = 3.5$ cm | | 3.0625 cm² |
| b) Rectangle, 5 cm by 90 cm | $\frac{1}{5}$ | |
| c) Triangle, $b = 4$ cm, $h = 6$ cm | 0.5 | |
| **⚙ Think Beyond** | | $\approx 3.14$ cm² |
| d) Circle, $r = 3$ cm | | |

**14.** What is the relationship between the scale factor $k$ and the area of an image when compared to the area of the original shape? Use three different shapes to demonstrate your answer.

**15.** Advertisers often state information in misleading ways. For example, a chocolate bar manufacturer reduced each of the dimensions of the "Dark Chocolate Delight" bar by $\frac{1}{4}$. An advertisement stated that the change in the amount of candy was not important since $\frac{1}{4}$ is very small. How would you respond?

**Think Beyond**

**16.** Imagine you have similar cubes. What relationship exists between the scale factor and the volume of the enlarged or reduced cube?

**Think Back**

**17.** Write these phrases as expressions.

  **a)** the quantity $y$ times eighteen subtracted from ninety-one

  **b)** the sum of the square of $r$ and five

  **c)** the quotient of $w$ and $c$

**18.** Let $w = {}^-4.2$ and $c = 8$. Evaluate Question 17c.

**19.** Use a protractor to determine the measure of each angle.

  **a)**    **b)**

  **c)** Define these terms: *right angle, acute angle, obtuse angle* and *straight angle.*

**20.** Isabelle is reviewing the different uses for variables. What does each of the following variables represent?

  **a)** $2x + 4 = y$     **b)** $5 - x = {}^-7$     **c)** $x + 0 = x$

**21.** Gary bought 14.8 gallons of gasoline for $33.90. At this rate, how much gas can Gary buy for $5? Round to the nearest hundredth of a gallon.

**Optional Technology Lesson for this section available in your eBook**

# Sum It Up

## Scale Drawings

A scale drawing is a drawing that represents a real object. Scale drawings that are larger than the original are called enlargements. Scale drawings that are smaller than the original are called reductions.

■ The scale compares each linear dimension on the scale drawing to the corresponding linear dimension on the original object (scale drawing : original).

■ A ratio of 3 : 1 indicates an enlargement. Each linear dimension in the drawing is 3 times as long as the corresponding original dimension. A ratio of 1 : 3 indicates a reduction. Each linear dimension in the drawing is $\frac{1}{3}$ times as long as the corresponding original dimension.

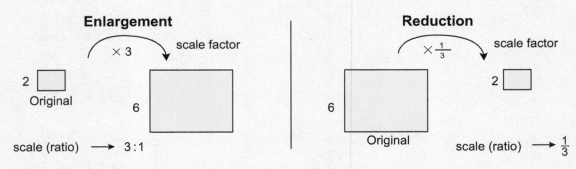

■ The scale factor is a single-number multiplier. It is the value of the scale. You multiply each dimension of the original drawing by a scale factor to create an enlargement or a reduction.

■ If the scale factor is 1, the image is congruent to the original.

■ The variable $k$ is commonly used to represent a scale factor. In the drawing below, $k = 2$. The perimeter of an enlargement or reduction is $k$ times the original perimeter. The area of an enlargement or reduction is $k^2$ times the original area.

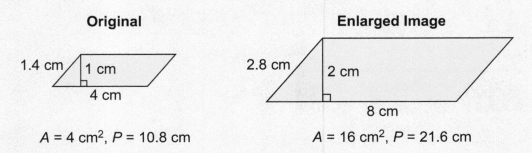

**Original**

$A = 4\ cm^2,\ P = 10.8\ cm$

**Enlarged Image**

$A = 16\ cm^2,\ P = 21.6\ cm$

# Similar Polygons

Similar polygons have corresponding congruent angles and corresponding sides that are in proportion. The symbol for "is similar to" is ~.

- *SIML* ~ *TRAP*.

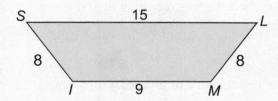 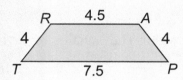

Corresponding angles are congurent: $\angle S \cong \angle T$, $\angle I \cong \angle R$, $\angle M \cong \angle A$, $\angle L \cong \angle P$

The symbol for "is congruent to" is $\cong$.

Corresponding sides are in proportion.

$$\frac{SI}{TR} = \frac{IM}{RA} = \frac{ML}{AP} = \frac{SL}{TP}$$

$$\frac{8}{4} = \frac{9}{4.5} = \frac{8}{4} = \frac{15}{7.5}$$

$$\frac{2}{1} = \frac{2}{1} = \frac{2}{1} = \frac{2}{1}$$

- *SIML* is an enlargement of *TRAP*. The scale is $2:1$. The scale factor is 2. Each dimension of *SIML* is twice the length of the corresponding dimension of *TRAP*. The area of *SIML* is 4 times the area of *TRAP*.

- *TRAP* is a reduction of *SIML*. The scale is $1:2$. The scale factor is $\frac{1}{2}$. Each dimension of *TRAP* is twice the length of the corresponding dimension of *SIML*. The area of *TRAP* is $\frac{1}{4}$ times the area of *SIML*.

# Ratio and Slope

■ The graph shows a proportional relationship between the *y*-values and the *x*-values. It is a direct variation graph.

■ As shown in the graph, the diagonals of similar rectangles, each with a vertex at the origin, form a straight line that is based on the ratio between length and width in the form of $y:x$.

■ The slope of the line in the graph below is 3, which is the value of the ratios of length to width. The equation of the line is $y = 3x$.

■ All points on the diagonal line can be written using the same $y:x$ ratio. The values of these ratios are the same because they are on the same line that passes through the origin.

■ The $y:x$ ratio for these rectangles is $3:1$, $6:2$ and $9:3$. All these ratios have a value of 3. The slope is equal to 3.

■ The slope of a direct variation graph is the ratio $y:x$ that describes the relationship between variables.

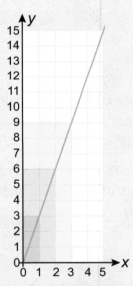

## MATHEMATICALLY SPEAKING

Do you know what these mathematical terms mean?

▶ congruent

▶ corresponding angles

▶ corresponding sides

▶ enlargement

▶ image

▶ linear dimension

▶ reduction

▶ scale

▶ scale drawing

▶ scale factor

▶ scale model

▶ similar

▶ slope

▶ symbol "≅"

▶ symbol "~"

# Study Guide

## Part 1. What did you learn?

1.  Molly used rectangle *ABCD* to create three similar rectangles.

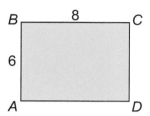

B ⎯⎯ 8 ⎯⎯ C
6
A ⎯⎯⎯⎯⎯ D

Molly gave only some of the information about rectangle *ABCD* and the three new rectangles she created. Copy and complete the table below.

| | Rectangle | Scale Factor from *ABCD* to New Rectangle | Dimensions of New Rectangle | Sketch of New Rectangle | Perimeter (cm) | Area (cm²) |
|---|---|---|---|---|---|---|
| **a.** | *ABCD* | 1 | 6 × 8 | 8 / 6 | | |
| **b.** | *EFGH* | | | 16 / 12 | | |
| **c.** | *IJKL* | | 3 × 4 | | | |
| **d.** | *MNOP* | 2.5 | | | | |

2. Explain what happens to the area of a rectangle when it is enlarged or reduced by a given scale factor.

3. A lesson in Marcia's math book contained a picture of two triangles. The text next to the picture read, "△ABC ≅ △FGH." What does this statement mean?

4. The drawing below has a scale of 1 : 16.

   a. Using your inch ruler, find the indicated height of the real donkey in inches and in feet.

   b. What scale factor was used to create the picture of the donkey?

   c. Imagine you want to make a drawing of a horse using the same scale. If a horse is 8 feet tall, how tall is the image of the horse? Explain how you determined this height.

5. Decide whether each of the statements is true or false.

   a. If two polygons are similar, they sometimes are congruent.

   b. A 12 × 18 rectangle is similar to a 2 × 3 rectangle.

   c. All rectangles are similar.

   d. If the scale factor from Rectangle A to Rectangle B is 3, then the area of Rectangle B is 3 times the area of Rectangle A.

**6.** Trapezoids *BOAT* and *FISH* are similar.

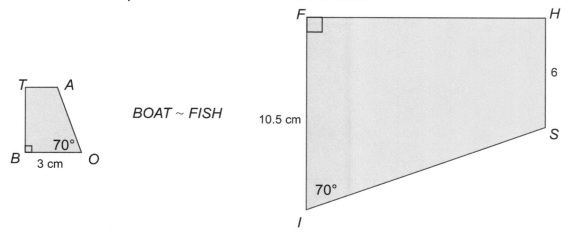

BOAT ~ FISH

**a.** List the four pairs of corresponding angles.

**b.** Form a ratio that compares each side length on *BOAT* to its corresponding side length on *FISH*. Are the ratios formed from each pair of corresponding sides equivalent?

**c.** Give the scale factor if *BOAT* is the original shape, and it is enlarged to form *FISH*.

**d.** Give the scale factor if *FISH* is the original shape, and it is reduced to form *BOAT*.

**7.** The tables below show the coordinates of points on three different lines. Use each table to find the slope of the line which is the value of the ratio that describes the relationship between the *y*-values and their corresponding *x*-values.

**a.** Line *A*

| x | 0 | 16 | 48 | 160 | 32 | 4 |
|---|---|----|----|-----|----|---|
| y | 0 | 4 | 12 | 40 | 8 | 1 |

**b.** Line *B*

| x | 0 | 4 | 16 | 20 | 2 | 14 |
|---|---|---|----|----|---|----|
| y | 0 | 6 | 24 | 30 | 3 | 21 |

**c.** Line *C*

| x | 0 | 2 | 4 | 6 | 22 | 40 |
|---|---|---|----|----|----|-----|
| y | 0 | 5 | 10 | 15 | 55 | 100 |

**8.** Examine the coordinate grid below.

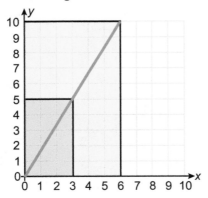

a. Find the slope of the line that passes through the diagonals of the rectangles.

b. Give the dimension of another rectangle whose diagonal would fall on the line drawn.

c. Give the dimensions of a rectangle whose diagonal would not fall on the line drawn.

**9.** Examine the scale drawings below. Then, use your ruler to answer the questions.

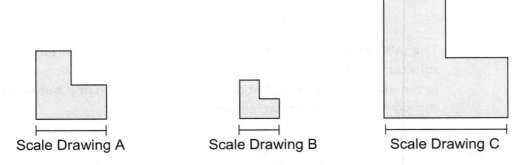

Scale Drawing A          Scale Drawing B          Scale Drawing C

a. If B is the original drawing, what is the scale factor for drawing A?

b. If A is the original drawing, what is the scale factor for drawing B?

c. If B is the original drawing, what is the scale factor for drawing C?

d. If C is the original drawing, what is the scale factor for drawing B?

10. Reem was asked the following multiple-choice question on a recent quiz.

> The scale factor from Rectangle A to Rectangle B is $\frac{1}{2}$.
> If the dimensions of Rectangle A are 3 × 4, which
> of the following are the dimensions of Rectangle B?
>
> **A.** 1 × 2                    **C.** 6 × 8
>
> **B.** 1.5 × 2                 **D.** $3\frac{1}{2} \times 4\frac{1}{2}$

Reem chose letter C but her answer was marked wrong. Why? What could you say or do to help Reem find the correct answer?

11. Bob's teacher asked him whether the shapes below were similar.

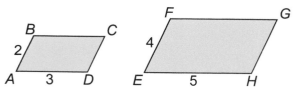

Figures not drawn to scale

Bob said, "Yes, the shapes are similar because they are the same shape, and only different sizes." Bob's teacher told him that his answer was not correct. Why? What doesn't Bob understand about similar shapes?

# Percent Sense

Percents are a useful way to convey information. The weather forecaster indicates there is a 10% chance of rain, an operation has a 95% success rate, banks advertise their interest rates as a percent and stores offer discounts of 25% to 50% on clothing at the end of each season. In this section you will deepen and extend your knowledge of percents and solve problems that involve percents.

### LESSON 3.1 Benchmark Percents

## ➡️ Start It Off

The following rectangle is called $R$.

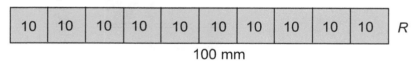

100 mm

1. Compare the following rectangles to $R$. What percent of $R$ is each?

   **a)**

   **b)**

   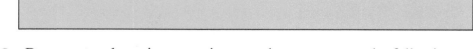

2. Draw rectangles using a centimeter ruler to represent the following. How long is each rectangle?

   **a)** 10% of $R$           **d)** 135% of $R$

   **b)** 110% of $R$          **e)** 5% of $R$

   **c)** 150% of $R$          **f)** 75% of $R$

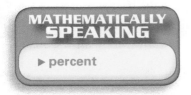

What do you think of when you hear the word *percent*? Some phrases that are associated with percent include *per 100*, *out of 100* and *for each 100*. These phrases make us think of a percent as a fraction.

A percent is also interpreted as a type of ratio where a number is compared to 100. When we think of percent as a comparison, it is easier to understand what percents greater than 100 represent. For example, 140% is a comparison of 140 to 100, and 300% represents 300 compared to 100.

# Using Benchmarks and Diagrams

Some percents are known as benchmark percents because you can use them to easily perform calculations or to make estimations. Some common benchmark percents are 1%, 10%, 20%, 25%, 50% and 75%.

You can use percent diagrams to solve problems that involve benchmark values. The top row of a percent diagram is for the numerical values and the bottom row is for the corresponding percents. Ziv drew the following diagram to solve this problem: 25% of the 60 people in the audience were children. How many children were in the audience?

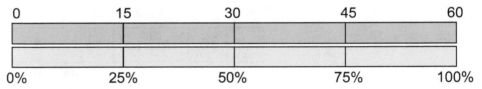

1. **a)** Why did Ziv divide the diagram into fourths?

   **b)** How can you use the diagram to find 25% of 60?

   **c)** How can you use the diagram to find 75% of 60?

   **d)** How would the diagram change if there were 400 people in the audience?

The benchmark 100% can help you solve problems where the percent is greater than 100.

- 120% is equal to 100% + 20%.

- 200% is twice the amount that equals 100%.

- 250% is equivalent to 100% + 100% + 50%.

Ziv made the diagram below to find 130% of 60. Remember that 130% equals 100% + 30%.

Ziv first drew a strip to show 100% and then drew 30% more. He knew that 130% of 60 was going to be greater than 60 because 100% of 60 = 60.

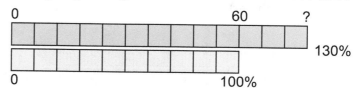

2. **a)** Make a sketch of this diagram and fill in the percent values in the bottom row and the numerical values in the top row.

   **b)** Did Ziv place the 60 in the correct place in the diagram? Why or why not?

   **c)** Why is the 100% divided into tenths?

   **d)** How can you use the diagram to determine the value of 10% of 60?

   **e)** Find 130% of 60.

3. **a)** In 2010, the population of Hopkinton was 185% of what it was in 1980. In 1980 the population was 10,000. Draw a diagram to illustrate this situation.

   **b)** What is 185% of 10,000?

To solve a problem, you often have choices of benchmark percents to use. Examine the different benchmarks that can be used to solve the following problem.

Kennedy earned a score of 80% on his math test of 40 problems. How many problems did he answer correctly?

- Use 1% as the benchmark.

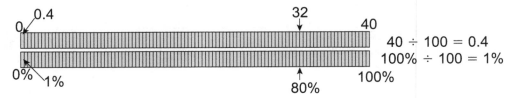

$40 \div 100 = 0.4$

$100\% \div 100 = 1\%$

100% of 40 problems is 40.

1% of 40 problems is 0.4          (Think: $100\% \div 100 = 1\%$ and $40 \div 100$ is 0.4)

80% of 40 is 32.                  (Think: $1\% \cdot 80 = 80\%$ and $0.4 \cdot 80 = 32$)

- Use 10% as the benchmark.

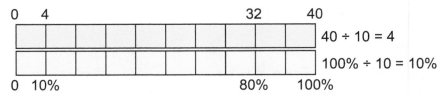

$40 \div 10 = 4$

$100\% \div 10 = 10\%$

100% of 40 problems is 40.

10% of 40 problems is 4.          (Think: $100\% \div 10 = 10\%$ and $40 \div 10 = 4$)

80% of 40 is 32.                  (Think: $10\% \cdot 8 = 80\%$ and $4 \cdot 8 = 32$)

- Use 20% as the benchmark.

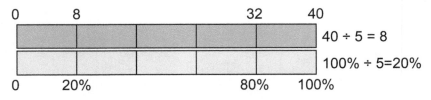

$40 \div 5 = 8$

$100\% \div 5 = 20\%$

100% of 40 problems is 40.

20% of 40 problems is 8.          (Think: $100\% \div 5 = 20\%$ and $40 \div 5 = 8$)

80% of 40 is 32.                  (Think: $20\% \cdot 4 = 80\%$ and $8 \cdot 4 = 32$)

Kennedy answered 32 out of 40 questions correctly.

Use benchmark percents to solve the following problems. Do not use a calculator.

4. Walter has been saving to buy a snowboard. Three brands are on sale and he plans to buy the cheapest one.

K2® Push Snowboard
$400
**SALE** 18% OFF !!! **SALE**

BAM Aviary Snowboard
$380
15% OFF !!!

Burton® Baron Snowboard
$410
20% OFF !!!

SNOWBOARDS
ON
SALE

R & J

**a)** How much is the savings on each snowboard?

**b)** What is the sale price of each snowboard?

5. Walter plans to use his new snowboard on Saturday. As a special promotion, the ski resort is offering two days of snowboarding for 160% of the cost of one day.

**a)** What does it mean to say that the price for two days is 160% of the price for one day? With the offer, will the price of two days of snowboarding be more or less than it would have been without the offer?

**b)** If the cost of a weekend lift ticket is $60 per day, how much will two days of lift tickets cost using this special deal?

# Sales and Discounts

When a store discounts merchandise, prices are often reduced by a certain percent. In order to be a savvy consumer, you need to be able to calculate sale prices.

6. Determine the new sale price with the discount. Use benchmark percents. (Remember that 5% is half of 10%.)

a)

Spaghetti Dinner $12.00
*All you can eat!*
**15% off**
*every* Monday!

b)

EVERYTHING MUST GO!
**40% savings**
JEANS WERE $49.99

c)

*TEENAGER DISCOUNT*
*Saturday only*
30%
discount on
$24.00 DVDs

7. a) Walter realized that he needs to buy snowboarding boots. A pair that originally cost $280 is on sale for 35% off. The salesperson commented, "You only have to pay 65% of $280." Was the salesperson correct? Explain.

b) What is the sale price of the boots?

There are two standard methods for solving percent-discount problems. You just used each in Questions 6 and 7.

**Example**

A CD that was $12 has been discounted by 15%. What is the new price of the CD?

**Method 1:** Use the percent the item is discounted to find the amount saved.

15% of $12 = $1.80

Subtract this amount from the original price: $12 − $1.80 = $10.20

**Method 2:** Determine the percent paid for the item by subtracting the percent discount from 100%.

100% − *percent discount* = *percent paid*: 100% − 15% = 85%

Use this percent to determine the sale price: 85% of $12 = $10.20

8. Use Method 2 to solve the following problems.

   a) A cookbook is on sale for 80% off the original price of $30. What is the sale price?

   b) Determine the price of a $145 cell phone that is discounted by 70%.

9. Solve using any method.

   a) Find the cost of a $180 MP3 player that is 15% off.

   b) A jacket that is priced at $50 is on sale for a savings of 40%. What is the sale price of the jacket?

 **Wrap It Up**

A student was absent and missed learning about benchmark percents. What are the most important ideas she should know? Be sure to include how to solve percent problems using benchmarks.

**MATHEMATICALLY SPEAKING**

▶ discount

▶ percent

Write
About It

Original Price $115
ON SALE

**30% off!**

1. There are two methods for finding the cost of an item on sale.

   a) Use both methods to find the sale price of the calculator.

   b) Explain which method you prefer and why.

2. At an auction, an antique toy car sold for 175% of the asking price of $85. What was the selling price of the toy car?

3. a) Your bones weigh about 15% of your entire body weight. If a person weighs 172 pounds, what is the weight of his or her bones?

   b) Bones are alive! 30% of bones is living tissue, 45% are mineral deposits (mainly calcium and phosphate) and the rest is water. Using the weight of the bones from Part a, how many pounds are water?

   c) If a person's bones weigh 15 pounds, what is his or her total weight?

4. Explain what each statement means?

   a) The entering class of freshmen is 150% the size of the previous class.

   b) 13% of the trees in the forest are insect-damaged.

   c) Santos received a grade of $\frac{1}{2}$% on his spelling quiz.

   d) The cost of the milk was 95% of the grocery bill.

   e) The CD is on sale at 25% off the original price.

   f) 60% of the books in the library are science fiction.

   g) At age 1, a baby's weight was 300% of her birth weight.

5. Use <, > or = to make true statements.

   a) 160% of 60 _____ 60

   b) 25% of 15 _____ 25% of 16

   c) 300% of 40 _____ 200% of 50

   d) 110% of 90 _____ 110% of 70

   e) $\frac{1}{2}$% of 12 _____ 1% of 12

   f) 150% of 24 _____ 100% of 36

6. Use benchmark percents to determine:

   a) 125% of 80

   b) 55% of 80

   c) 90% of 80

   d) 650% of 80

   e) 7% of 80

7. Determine the sale price of the following items.

   a) Jean jacket for $120, on sale for 25% off

   b) Designer T-shirts for $39, on sale for 10% off

   c) $84 jeans reduced by $\frac{1}{3}$

   d) Sweatshirts originally $48, on sale for 40% off

8. At a restaurant, the custom is to leave a 15% tip for the waiter or waitress. Use benchmark percents to find the amount of tip to leave for a $56 meal.

9. Most states have sales tax. If a state has a sales tax of 5%, how much must you pay in tax on a purchase worth:

   a) $1

   b) $7

   c) $10

   d) $37.50

10. A shopkeeper purchased handbags for $25 each. He sold them for 250% of what he paid. What was the price the shopkeeper charged for a handbag?

11. Solve the following puzzle:

   Take the last 25% of *burp*.

   Take the first $33\frac{1}{3}$% of *errand*.

   Take the last letter of the first 50% of *describe*.

   Take the last 40% of *presidents*.

   Put the letters together in order. What does it spell?

12. A research study showed that many people are tired or nod off on the job. Based on a random sample of 1,000 people, the study found:

   • 29% of the sample had fallen asleep or become very sleepy at work

   • 12% of the sample had been late to work because of sleepiness

   How many of the 1,000 people sampled fell asleep at work or were late because of sleepiness?

---

**Dining Check**

| | |
|---|---|
| steak | 26.00 |
| salad | 8.00 |
| dessert sampler | 22.00 |
| total | 56.00 |

*Thank you!*

13. Imagine that there are 60 students in the school band. Write three different percent problems about the band that can be solved using this percent diagram.

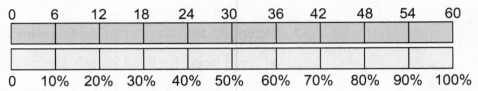

14. List words and phrases that indicate an item is on sale.

15. Imagine building a rectangular prism with dimensions 5 in. by 5 in. by 4 in. out of one-inch cubes.

   a) How many cubes are needed to build the rectangular prism?

   b) Imagine dipping the entire prism into red paint so that all 6 faces are red. Now imagine breaking the prism up into the small cubes. Fill in the table to show the percent of the small cubes that have 0, 1, 2 or 3 red faces.

| | 0 red faces | 1 red face | 2 red faces | 3 red faces |
|---|---|---|---|---|
| Number of Cubes | | | | |
| Percent | | | | |

   c) Imagine painting other rectangular prisms with a volume of 100 cubic units so that all 6 faces are red and then breaking these prisms into small unit cubes. Do all these rectangular prisms have the same percents of small cubes with 0, 1 and 2 red faces? Investigate by examining examples.

16. Whitman had 20 apples to use to make apple tarts. Each tart uses $\frac{3}{4}$ of an apple. How many tarts can he make?

17. Determine the solution of $-3.5 = 0.75r$.

    **A.** $-2\frac{3}{4}$

    **B.** $-2\frac{5}{8}$

    **C.** $-4\frac{1}{4}$

    **D.** $-4\frac{2}{3}$

18. Imagine this pattern continues: $125, 25, 5, 1, \frac{1}{5}, \ldots$

    **a)** Find the next three terms.

    **b)** Write a rule for finding the next term that uses multiplication.

19. Write a problem that can be represented by the equation $g - 23.65 = 63.95$.

20. Use all the digits, 1, 2, 4 and 6, to form four-digit numbers that are divisible by 4.

# LESSON 3.2 Percent Equations

## Start It Off

1. Explain why a percent is a ratio.

2. Kit, a 7th grade boy, is 164 cm tall. Use benchmark percents to find:

   **a)** 50% of Kit's height      **e)** 10% of Kit's height

   **b)** 25% of Kit's height      **f)** 1% of Kit's height

   **c)** 12.5% of Kit's height     **g)** 37.5% of Kit's height

   **d)** 75% of Kit's height      **h)** 87.5% of Kit's height

3. Explain how you determined the answers to Questions 2g and 2h.

About 73% of the 7th grade class of 182 pupils at Walter Reed Middle School participates in after-school activities. In comparison, 86% of the 150 8th graders at the same school are in after-school activities. The principal of the school plans to give out certificates of participation to these students.

1. Work with a partner to determine the number of certificates the principal needs for each grade. Be ready to present your work and an explanation of your solution method to the class.

You probably found that there are many ways to solve percent problems like this one. Using benchmark percents and diagrams are useful methods but are not always the most efficient.

# Solving Percent Equations

Let's examine some solution methods for finding 73% of 182. 73% is not a common benchmark percent, but there are a number of ways to find the value of 73% of 182. Recall that we can represent percents as decimals and as ratios.

---
**Example**

Since 73% of 182 is equal to 0.73 of 182, one way to find this amount is to use multiplication.

**Method 1:** *Write the percent as a decimal and solve an equation.*

$$73\% \text{ of } 182 = n$$
$$0.73 \cdot 182 = n$$
$$132.86 = n$$
$$n \approx 133 \text{ students}$$

**Method 2:** *Write the percent as a ratio and solve a proportion.*

$$\frac{73}{100} = \frac{n}{182}$$
$$73 \cdot 182 = 100 \cdot n$$
$$\frac{73 \cdot 182}{100} = n$$
$$132.86 = n$$
$$n \approx 133 \text{ students}$$

---

2. Examine the two solution methods.

   **a)** Explain each of the methods.

   **b)** What do these two methods have in common?

   **c)** Compare the equations $\frac{73 \cdot 182}{100} = n$ and $0.73 \cdot 182 = n$. How are these equations related?

3. Luis used a benchmark of 1% of 182 to solve 73% of 182. He multiplied $1.82 \cdot 73$. What does the 1.82 in the expression represent? Why does this expression give the same answer as the two equations in Question 2c?

4. Which of the three methods above do you like best? Why?

5. **a)** Write three different equations that can be used to find 86% of 150.

   **b)** What is 86% of 150?

Marilyn's dad stopped to put some gasoline in the truck because it was "on empty." 7.8 gallons cost over $25.00! When he looked at the fuel gauge, he noticed that it was only at 30% of the capacity of the tank. He said, "I wonder how many gallons the tank will hold."

**6. a)** Copy the percent diagram for this situation. How are the values in the problem above represented on the diagram?

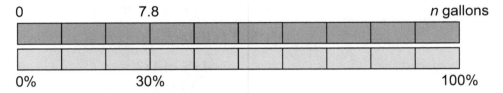

**b)** How many gallons does each 10% section represent?

**c)** How many gallons of gasoline will the truck hold when filled to capacity?

**d)** If 30% of a number, $n$, is 7.8, write a corresponding equation and solve for $n$.

**e)** At $3.30 per gallon, how much would it cost to fill the truck's empty tank?

**7.** Examine this newspaper report.

> # Latest Election Polls
>
> The senator's showing in yesterday's primary election indicates that he may be our next president. He received 45% of the vote, or 23,580 votes. No one is sure why so many people voted yesterday. The turnout was high—a total of 49,518 voters. Voters that cast their ballot for the senator cited his excellent reputation for keeping campaign promises and his commitment to lowering taxes as a part of their reason for voting for him in this election. General elections for the presidency, as well as various state, county and local officials will be held on November 5th at various locations throughout the city. More information will be sent

**a)** Sketch a percent diagram to represent this situation. Divide the diagram to show 5% intervals. How many people does each 5% interval represent?

**b)** What was the total number of votes in the election? Explain how you used the value of 5% of the votes to find 100% of the votes.

**c)** Write an equation to represent this situation. Let $n$ represent the total number of votes.

## Wrap It Up

In this lesson, you have solved percent problems. Diagrams can be used to help make sense of the relationships within each problem. Then, equations can be written to model and solve the problem. For each problem below, draw a diagram and write an equation. Discuss your thinking with your classmates.

- Elger joined the school track team. Yesterday Elger didn't feel well so he only ran 2.8 miles, 25% of the normal long-distance run. What is the length of the run?

- Eight percent of the freshmen at Bentley High School joined the marching band. There are 275 students in the freshman class. How many freshmen joined the band?

# On Your Own

**Write About It**

1. You have learned several methods for solving percent problems. Describe at least three different methods. How do you determine which method to use? Give examples to illustrate your points.

2. Monica deposited $1,200 in the bank. She was paid simple interest of 4.75% per year. This means her $1,200 increased by 4.75% after 1 year. How much money did Monica receive in interest in 1 year?

3. Beatriz has a babysitting job every Saturday. She decides to save 15%, or $4.50, of her weekly salary. How much does Beatriz make babysitting each week?

4. Every middle school student at Sutton Junior High School has to take a geography test. Seven out of 200 students failed the test. What percent passed the test?

5. Mr. Rodriguez spent $78 on groceries. He spent 28% on fruits and vegetables. How much money did Mr. Rodriquez spend on products other than fruits and vegetables?

6. Examine the percent diagrams below and determine the unknown values.

    a)
    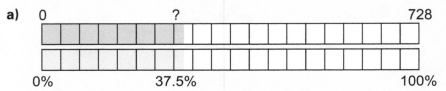

    b)
    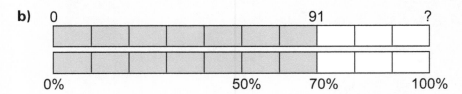

7. Create a percent problem and find the solution. Draw and shade a percent diagram. Give your problem to a classmate to solve.

    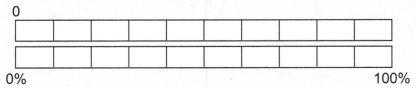

8. At a restaurant, one customer left a $16.00 tip on an $82.90 check. Another customer left a $15.00 tip on a $73.50 bill. Estimate the percent of the check each tip represents. Explain your mental strategy.

9. The lowest listed online price for a particular video game is $17.25. The website claims that you save 65%. If the online company's claim is true, what was the original cost of the game?

10. Preston paid $18.00 for a new video game. The price was advertised as 80% of the actual cost. How much did the video game cost before the discount?

11. The World Health Organization predicts that 125,000 people die each year from snakebites. If 20% of snakebites are fatal, how many snakebites occur each year?

12. a) Did you know that 70% of Americans have visited Disneyland® or Disney World®? The 2008 population of the United States was 298,444,215. Approximately how many people had visited at least one of the theme parks?

   b) Every day, 7% of Americans eat at McDonald's®. Using the U.S. population figure from Part a, about how many people ate at McDonald's® each day?

   c) Find the current population of the United States. How many people now eat at McDonald's® every day?

   d) Find interesting scientific facts using reference books or the Internet. Use some of these facts to write five interesting percent problems for your classmates. Solve your problems.

13. Ernie said, "The formula $V = Bh$ can be used to find the volume of prisms and cylinders because you can stack up the bases." What do you think Ernie means?

14. Place these decimals in order from least to greatest.

   a) 0.235; 0.2503; 0.25; 0.2350

   b) 4.1901; 4.191; 4.0199; 4.02

15. What is one-half of two-thirds of 180?

16. On Saturday, Brushes and Rollers paint store had 29 customers. The table shows the amount each customer spent. Use this information to answer the questions that follow.

| Total Amount of Purchases in Dollars | Number of Sales |
|---|---|
| 0.01–15.00 | 8 |
| 15.01–25.00 | 3 |
| 25.01–35.00 | 5 |
| 35.01–45.00 | 2 |
| 45.01–55.00 | 2 |
| 55.01–65.00 | 5 |
| 65.01 + | 4 |

   a) How many customers spent more than $45.00?

   b) Can you determine the median or the mode of this data set? Explain.

17. Sketch and label the following solids using the terms *base*, *diameter*, *lateral surface*, *edge*, *face*, *radius* and *vertex*.

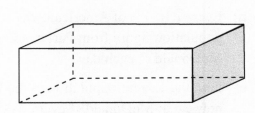
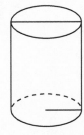

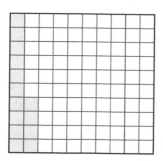

# LESSON 3.3 Determining Percents

➡️ **Start It Off**

1. Tell what percent of each diagram is shaded.

   a)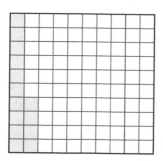

   d)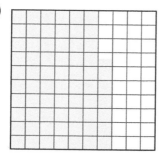

   b)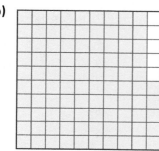

   e)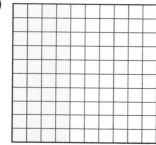

   c)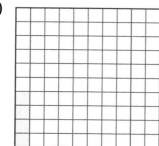

2. Express each percent in Question 1 as a decimal and as a simplified fraction.

3. Eileen thinks that $\frac{3}{5}$, 0.6 and 60% are three different numbers. Roberto thinks that these are the same number. What do you think?

Food contains proteins, carbohydrates, fats, water, vitamins and minerals. The U.S. government makes dietary recommendations that include limiting the amount of fat in one's diet to less than 30% of a day's calories. About 15% of a day's calories should come from proteins, and approximately 55% of all daily calories should come from carbohydrates.

**1. a)** Rewrite each of the percents in the paragraph above as a fraction and a decimal.

**b)** Describe the steps you take to change percents to fractions and percents to decimals.

Information provided on cereal boxes includes the number of grams of nutrients in each serving. Examine the data provided for the following cereals.

| | Nutrients (in grams) per Serving | | | | |
|---|---|---|---|---|---|
| | **Krispy Rice** | **Lightly Frosted Shredded Wheat** | **Crunch of Nature** | **Cinnamon Crunchy Toast** | **Cereal O's** |
| Protein (g) | 2 | 4 | 5 | 2 | 3 |
| Sugar (g) | 3 | 12 | 17 | 10 | 1 |
| Complex Carbohydrates (g) | 25 | 27 | 19 | 12 | 18 |
| Fiber (g) | 0 | 5 | 4 | 1 | 3 |
| Fat (g) | 0 | 1 | 3 | 3 | 2 |
| Other (g) | 3 | 1 | 7 | 2 | 3 |
| Total (g) | 33 | 50 | 55 | 30 | 30 |

Percents are especially useful when trying to compare the proportion of nutrients in two or more cereals. Notice that most of the cereals in the chart have a different total number of grams in one serving.

**2.** Tahir thinks that Crunch of Nature will be the sweetest-tasting cereal since it has the most grams of sugar, but Fabian disagrees with this reasoning. What might be Fabian's reasons for disagreeing?

**3. a)** For each brand, determine what fraction of the total number of grams is sugar.

**b)** Represent these fractions as percents. Which cereal has the highest proportion of sugar per serving?

**c)** Represent these percents as decimals. What method did you use?

**d)** Is it fair to state that about 1 out of every 3 bites you take of Cinnamon Crunchy Toast is sugar? Explain.

**e)** Why might you want to pay attention to the amount of sugar you eat at breakfast?

4. **a)** List the cereals from least to greatest in terms of the number of grams of protein.

   **b** Calculate the percent of protein in a serving for each brand of cereal. How does your list compare with Part a?

   **c)** Why might you want to pay attention to the proportion of nutrients in your breakfast cereal?

5. **a)** What percent of a serving of Lightly Frosted Shredded Wheat cereal is fat? Show your work.

   **b)** Make up your own percent question using the cereal data.

## Percents Less Than 1%

Percents such as $\frac{1}{4}$% and 0.2% represent small portions of a whole. How do you make sense of percents less than 1%? Remember that the percent sign indicates a comparison to 100.

---
**Example**

How can you determine $\frac{1}{4}$% of 20?

**Method 1:** Use benchmark percents.

$$\div 4 \left( \begin{array}{l} 1\% \text{ of } 20 = 0.2 \\ \frac{1}{4}\% \text{ of } 20 = n \end{array} \right) \div 4 \qquad n = 0.05$$

**Method 2:** Write a proportion and scale down.

$$\div 5$$
$$\frac{\frac{1}{4}}{100} = \frac{n}{20} \qquad \frac{1}{4} \div 5 = \frac{1}{20}, n = \frac{1}{20} \text{ or } 0.05$$
$$\div 5$$

**Method 3:** Write a proportion and use cross products.

$$\frac{\frac{1}{4}}{100} = \frac{n}{20}$$
$$100n = \frac{1}{4} \cdot 20$$
$$100n = 5$$
$$n = 5 \div 100$$
$$n = 0.05$$

---

Sometimes when solving problems, it is useful to write a percent as a decimal.

 **Let's Review**

To write a percent as a decimal, we compare it to 100.

$$14\% = \frac{14}{100} = 0.14$$

$$176\% = \frac{176}{100} = 1.76$$

$$3\% = \frac{3}{100} = 0.03$$

Representing percents that are less than 1% as decimals requires careful attention to the placement of the decimal point. It is easy to confuse representations.

**6. a)** Do 33%, $\frac{1}{3}$ and $\frac{1}{3}\%$ represent the same rational number? Why or why not?

**b)** Explain what 0.75% means.

To write percents that are less than 1% as decimals, first rewrite the fractional part of the percent as a decimal. Then because it is a percent, write a ratio that compares the percent to 100. You can then use division to find the value of the ratio.

$$\frac{1}{4}\% = 0.25\% \qquad 0.25\% = \frac{0.25}{100} = 0.25 \div 100 = 0.0025$$

$$\frac{1}{2}\% = 0.5\% \qquad 0.5\% = \frac{0.5}{100} = 0.5 \div 100 = 0.005$$

---

**Example**

Another way to find $\frac{1}{4}\%$ of 20 is to represent the percent as a decimal, and then write and solve an equation. $\frac{1}{4}\%$ is equivalent to 0.25%, or 0.0025 as a decimal.

**Method 4:** Write an equation.

$$\frac{1}{4}\% \text{ of } 20 = n$$
$$0.25\% \text{ of } 20 = n$$
$$0.0025 \text{ of } 20 = n$$
$$0.0025 \cdot 20 = n$$
$$0.05 = n$$

---

The chart below lists some information about one serving of oatmeal. The % Daily Value tells you what percent of specific nutrients you will get by eating one serving of this oatmeal, based on a 2,000-calorie diet.

| Oatmeal | Protein | Fat | Calcium | Vit. K | Vit. E | Fiber |
|---|---|---|---|---|---|---|
| % Daily Value | 14% | 5% | 2% | 0.5% | 0.8% | 33% |

**7.  a)** Make a copy of the grid below and illustrate the percent of vitamin K by shading. How does this percent compare to the percent of calcium?

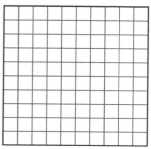

**b)** Write each percent in the chart as a fraction and as a decimal.

**c)** There is 0.13 gram of potassium in one 40-gram serving of oatmeal. What percent of oatmeal is potassium?

**8.  a)** About how many servings of oatmeal would you need to eat to get the daily recommendations for fiber?

**b)** About how many servings of oatmeal would you need to eat to get the daily recommendations for vitamin E?

**rap It Up**

Ms. Schuster, a 7th grade teacher, noticed that many students were confusing 5%, 0.5% and $\frac{1}{2}$. How are these numbers different and why might students confuse them?

**Write About It**

1. You just won $200 and plan to give some of it to charity. How does the amount of money you donate change as the percent changes from 100% to 10% to 1% to 0.1% to 0.01%? Describe any patterns.

2. Sales tax is tax you pay on the price of items purchased. The percent of sales tax differs by state. Determine the cost of a bicycle priced at $189 with a 7.25% sales tax.

3. a) Measure your height in centimeters (or convert your height in inches to centimeters by multiplying by 2.54).

   b) Measure the length of your foot in centimeters. What percent of your height is the length of your foot?

   c) Measure the length of your head from chin to top in centimeters. What percent of your height is the length of your head?

Use the chart on breakfast choices from a local diner and a calculator to answer Questions 4–6.

| | Total Calories | Calories from Fat | Cholesterol (mg) | Sodium |
|---|---|---|---|---|
| Pancakes and Bacon | 470 | 81 | 25 | 1,135 |
| Eggs and Muffin | 290 | 99 | 226 | 740 |
| Double Egg Platter | 710 | 414 | 457 | 1,700 |
| Scrambled Egg Special | 768 | 477 | 412 | 1,271 |
| Apple Bran Muffin | 190 | 0 | 0 | 230 |
| Apple Cinnamon Danish | 390 | 117 | 19 | 305 |

4. Which of the breakfasts listed above has the highest percent of calories due to fat?

5. Health authorities now advise limiting sodium (salt) to 3,300 milligrams or less a day. Give the range of percents of salt from these breakfast choices.

6. Cholesterol is used in the body for cell development. Too much can accumulate on artery walls. Government agencies recommend that cholesterol intake be limited to 300 milligrams or less a day. A man on a low-cholesterol diet has a Double Egg Platter and states, "I have only used up 65% of my cholesterol allotment for today." If you were his doctor, how do you reply?

7. Use the Internet to gather information about the percent of fat in different lunch or dinner entrees. Develop a set of percent questions for your classmates that would help them learn about healthy choices in terms of fat content when they eat popular foods.

8. Multivitamin brands must list the percents of the recommended daily value for all vitamins and minerals contained in each tablet. One brand states that each tablet supplies 417% of the recommended daily value of vitamin B12. Write this percent as a fraction and decimal. Explain what this percent means.

9. The recommended percent of chlorine in pool water is 0.2%. If 3,500 gallons of water are used to fill a public pool, how many gallons of chlorine should be added?

10. a) Most 7th graders get about 8 hours of sleep each night during the week and 10 hours per night on the weekends. What percent of a week are most 7th graders asleep?

    b) What percent of the past week were you asleep?

11. People in Thailand watch an average of 22.4 hours per week of television. One reason is that 80% of Thai people get all their news from television. What percent of the week does the average Thai citizen spend watching television?

12. About 76% of the 300,000 people in Iceland used the Internet in 2007. Approximately how many people used the Internet in Iceland that year?

13. Change these decimals to percents.

    a) 0.003                c) 0.0015

    b) 0.125                d) 2.23

14. Change these mixed numbers and fractions to percents. Round to the tenths place.

    a) $40\frac{1}{40}$          c) $\frac{7}{10,000}$

    b) $3\frac{5}{8}$            d) $\frac{17}{250}$

15. About 60% of the pupils in a mathematics class are boys. If there are 12 girls in the class, how many boys are in the class?

16. Compare the following statements: "One serving of food X provides $\frac{1}{3}$ of your daily protein needs" and "One serving of food X provides $\frac{1}{3}$% of your daily protein needs."

 **Think Beyond**

17. Randy has a stamp collection. 20% of his stamps are from overseas. Of the stamps that are from overseas, 25% are from Asia. What percent of the total number of stamps are from Asia?

**Think Back**

18. Find three $(x, y)$ pairs that make this inequality true. Use positive and negative integers: $\frac{1}{4} \cdot x - 7 < y$.

19. Sterling's car is $15\frac{2}{3}$ feet long. If Sterling wants to make a model of his car using a scale factor of $\frac{1}{64}$, how long will the model be?

20. A quart of red paint fits inside a tin can that is $4\frac{3}{4}$ inches tall with a diameter of 4 inches. How much paint can fit in this can? Round your answer to the nearest tenth of a cubic inch.

   **A.** 19 in.³      **C.** 59.7 in.³

   **B.** 9.5 in.³     **D.** 238.6 in.³

21. What is a rational number? Give examples to support your definition.

22. Find the explicit rule for the total number of triangles in Stage $s$ if two triangles (in the form of a diamond) are added to each successive stage.

Stage 1          Stage 2          Stage 3

## LESSON 3.4 Changing Percents

### ➡️ Start It Off

1. Write these decimals as percents.

   **a)** 0.0245      **d)** 0.16

   **b)** 0.0098      **e)** 2.009

   **c)** 1.24

2. Write these percents as decimals and fractions.

   **a)** 3%      **d)** 43%

   **b)** 927.5%      **e)** 0.7%

   **c)** $\frac{3}{4}$%

3. Simplify these fractions to find equivalent fractions.

   **a)** $\frac{16}{200}$      **d)** $\frac{13}{39}$

   **b)** $\frac{28}{32}$      **e)** $\frac{36}{54}$

   **c)** $\frac{56}{49}$

4. Write the fractions in Questions 3b and 3e as percents.

## Percent Increase and Percent Decrease

When students watch television excessively, they spend less time doing other activities. Studies have found that students who watch 6 or more hours of television every day, on average, score lower on national mathematics assessment exams.

The good news is that more students are watching less television. In 1991, about 20% of middle school students watched 1 hour or less of television each weekday. But in 2004, approximately 27% of middle school students watched 1 hour or less! How much television do you think the average middle school student watches today?

**1.** Write down three facts from the paragraphs above.

Teachers at the Washington Middle School conducted a survey. In 2008, they asked 8th graders how many hours of television they watched, and then they asked the same students again in 2010 when they were in high school.

| Hours of TV Watching on an Average Weekday | Number of Pupils in 2008 | Number of Pupils in 2010 |
|---|---|---|
| 1 hour or less | 114 | 144 |
| Between 1–3 hours | 161 | 168 |
| 3 or more hours | 95 | 58 |
| Total | 370 | 370 |

2. Calculate the percents of students in 2008 who watched television for 1 hour or less, between 1–3 hours and for 3 or more hours.

3. Calculate the percents of students in 2010 who watched television for 1 hour or less, between 1–3 hours and for 3 or more hours.

4. Describe the changes in television viewing between 2008 and 2010. Why might these changes have occurred?

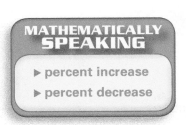

**MATHEMATICALLY SPEAKING**

▶ percent increase

▶ percent decrease

It is sometimes useful to examine how a value has increased or decreased. The percent increase or percent decrease is a multiplicative comparison between the amount of change and the original amount. The number of students who watch 1 hour or less of TV has increased from 114 to 144; 30 is the amount of change. Compare the amount of change to the original value to determine a percent.

---

**Example**

What is the percent increase in the number of students watching television 1 hour or less on a weekday from 2008 to 2010?

There are 30 more students watching television 1 hour or less in 2010 than in 2008.

$$144 - 114 = 30$$

To determine the percent of increase, compare 30 (the difference) to the original number of 114 students.

**Method 1:** Form a proportion and solve.

$$\frac{30}{114} = \frac{n}{100} \qquad n \approx 26.3 \qquad \text{so about } 26\%$$

**Method 2:** Represent the fraction as a decimal and then as a percent.

$$\frac{30}{114} \approx 0.263 \qquad 0.263 \approx 26\%$$

There was about a 26% increase.

Notice that the percent of students who watch television 1 hour or less on average is different than the percent that this value increased. To calculate percent increase or percent decrease, you compare the change to the original amount, not the total.

| 2008 | 2010 | Percent Change |
|---|---|---|
| $\frac{114}{370} \approx 31\%$ | $\frac{144}{370} \approx 39\%$ | $\frac{30}{114} \approx 26\%$ |

5. **a)** Imagine that in 2010, 228 of the 370 students said they watched 1 hour or less of TV on weekdays. What is the percent increase from 2008 in that situation?

   **b)** Explain what information this percent increase provides.

6. What is the percent increase in the number of students who watched television between 1–3 hours from 2008 to 2010? Compare the difference to the original 2008 value.

You can also calculate percent decrease, which is a ratio that compares the amount of decrease to the original value.

7. What is the percent decrease in the number students who watched 3 hours or more of TV from 2008 to 2010?

# Sales, Markups and Markdowns

Sometimes stores offer multiple discounts. The jacket above was reduced by 50%, and then the new price was marked down by another 50%.

8. **a)** What is the final sale price of the jacket?

   **b)** When Janet went to buy the jacket, a woman was arguing with the clerk that 50% off plus an additional 50% off meant that the jacket was free! How would you explain that this was not true?

   **c)** A discount of 50% followed by an additional 50% off is equivalent to what percent discount?

Did you know that stores buy items at "cost" and then increase the price by a certain percent before selling them? This increase is called a **markup**. If T-Shirt Haven buys shirts from a manufacturer for $10 each and increases the price 100%, the store sells each shirt for $20.

Another way of thinking about this is that the shirts are now 200% of the original cost (100% original price + 100% markup). Some stores apply huge markups to items, while others use a much smaller percent.

9. Find the new price.

**a)** A TV from the manufacturer costs a store $120. The store then marks up the price by 425%. What is the new price?

**b)** A bracelet that costs the store $15 is marked up $33\frac{1}{3}$%. What is the new price?

**c)** A pair of sneakers that a shoe store purchases for $6 are marked up 1,000%. What is the new price of the sneakers?

10. How are markups related to percent increase?

Because so many companies and stores increase the price of their goods by large markups, they can afford to put items on sale. Consider a coat that costs a store $40. The store sells the coat at a price that is a 150% markup of the cost of $40. At end of the month, if the coat hasn't sold, it is put on sale for 20% off. Sometimes the "percent off" the item on sale is called a **markdown**.

---

**Example**

What is the final price of the coat? How much money does the store make on one coat following the markup and markdown process?

**Step 1:** Determine the original selling price of the coat with a 150% markup.
Find 250% of 40 (cost: 100% of 40 + markup: 150% of 40)
$2.50 \cdot 40 = 100$
The selling price of the coat is $100. The markup was $60 (150% of 40).

**Step 2:** Determine the sale price of the coat with a 20% discount.
Find 80% of 100 (20% off means you pay 80%)
$0.80 \cdot 100 = 80$
The sale price of the coat is $80.
The store makes a profit of $40 on each coat, even when the coat is "on sale."

---

11. A DVD player costs an electronics store $42. It is marked up 200%. During the annual sale, the price is marked down 40%. What is the final marked-down price of the DVD player?

12. If the original price of an item is first marked up 25% and then that price is marked down 25%, is the final cost the same as the original price? Show with an example why or why not.

rap It Up

Sales, markups and markdowns are used extensively in retail businesses. Explain what each of these terms means and how they are used to price items.

MATHEMATICALLY
SPEAKING

▶ markdown

▶ markup

▶ percent decrease

▶ percent increase

 Write About It

1. Explain to a classmate how to determine the new price of an item following a markup. Find the new price of a $60 baseball game ticket that is being resold at a 400% markup. Use diagrams, words, numbers or percent bars in your explanation.

2. The price of gas jumped from $2.80 to $3.80 per gallon in a nine-month period. By what percent did the price increase?

3. What percent of 2 hours is 12 minutes?

4. A house bought for $60,000 in 1980 sold for $400,000 in 2000. What is the percent of increase?

5. Cars lose their value very quickly. A car worth $12,000 one year is only valued at $8,000 the next. What is the percent decrease?

6. At the end of the summer, a store decided to put their tank tops on sale. A tank top that originally cost $12.50 was priced at $7.99.

   a) What is the percent of decrease for this item? Round to the nearest percent.

   b) The store put up this sign: "Sale on TANK TOPS. Save 64%." Is this sign accurate? If yes, explain why. If no, change it so it is correct.

7. Children, on average, spend 12% of the week watching TV, playing video games or using a computer. How many hours are children engaged in these types of activities?

8. a) George W. Bush received 50,460,110 votes in the 2000 election and 62,040,606 votes in the 2004 election. What percent increase of votes did he receive in 2004 compared to the votes he received in 2000?

   b) If there were a total of 105,405,100 votes cast in the 2000 election, what percent of the votes did George W. Bush receive?

   c) If there were a total of 122,294,978 votes cast in the 2004 election, what percent of the votes did George W. Bush receive?

9. Did you know that the area of the Sahara Desert in Africa is 3,500,000 million square miles, and only 30% of the desert is actually covered in sand? Gravel and rock cover the rest of the surface. Use benchmark percents to calculate the number of square miles that are covered in sand.

10. During the month of March, one store offers a digital camera for 25% off the regular price of $199.99. On St. Patrick's Day, the store holds a one-day sale and slashes prices on all merchandise an additional 15%. What is the price of the camera on St. Patrick's Day?

11. Imagine that you manage your school store. The store pays a supplier 5¢ for each pencil and 70¢ for each notebook.

   a) Determine a reasonable selling price for pencils and notebooks so the store will make a profit.

   b) Now that you have a price for your merchandise, determine the percent markup for each item.

12. Crazy Sneakers is a new store whose owners decide to constantly advertise sales in order to draw customers into the store. They plan to mark up all sneakers by 500% and then put them on sale for 30% off.

   a) Give the sale price for sneakers that cost the store $8.50 and for sneakers that cost the store $4.75.

   b) Crazy Sneakers wants to make a profit of $50 on an exclusive brand of basketball sneakers. If it costs the store $10 to buy the sneakers and they plan to sell them to customers for 30% off, what markup is needed?

13. On one sale rack, a pair of pants had been marked down three times: by 15%, then by 30% and then again by 50%. If the pants were originally priced at $45, what is the final sale price? Round to the nearest cent.

**14.** An $85 television is marked up 250% and is later put on sale for 40% off. What is the final price of the TV?

**15.** If you want to mark up an item by 25% but then mark it down so it is priced at the original price, what markdown should you use? Explain your reasoning and give examples with different starting amounts.

**16.** Idina is drawing nets of geometric solids. Sketch a net of a rectangular prism. A cylinder. A square pyramid.

**17.** Write a multiplication expression that is equal to $-48 \div 4$. Then, solve the expression.

**18.** Evaluate $\left( \dfrac{-13 + 6}{5} + \dfrac{8}{-2 - 3} \right)^2$.

**19.** Find $d$. Show your work and write your answer as a fraction and as a decimal.

$$-12d + 8 = 24$$

**20. a)** Explain how to use partitioning to locate $\dfrac{11}{32}$ on the following number line.

**b)** How many fractions are between $\dfrac{11}{32}$ and $\dfrac{12}{32}$? Explain your answer.

Optional Technology Lesson for this section available in your eBook

# Sum It Up

## Percent–Fraction–Decimal Relationships

■ Percents are ratios that compare a number to 100. Percents that are less than 1%, such as 0.25% or $\frac{3}{4}$%, represent a small proportion of a quantity. Percents that are greater than 100%, such as 150% or 400%, represent a quantity whose value is greater than the original.

| | | |
|---|---|---|
| 1% of 100 is 1. | 0.25% of 100 is 0.25. | 0.25% of 5 is 0.0125. |
| 100% of 100 is 100. | 150% of 100 is 150. | 150% of 5 is 7.5. |

■ Percents can be rewritten as fractions or decimals. Benchmark percents are those percents that are easily converted to fractions or decimals and are helpful when computing mentally.

25% is equivalent to $\frac{1}{4}$.

50% is equivalent to $\frac{1}{2}$.

75% is equivalent to $\frac{3}{4}$.

1% is equivalent to 0.01.

10% is equivalent to 0.1.

20% is equivalent to $\frac{1}{5}$.

## Find the Percent of a Number

There are several methods for finding the percent of a number. Consider the example below:

Camile was overjoyed that buying a ticket on the day of a performance cost her only 55% of the original $80 price. How much was her ticket?

■ Use benchmark values.

50% of 80 is 40 and 5% of 80 is 4.
55% of 80 is 44.
A ticket costs $44.

■ Rewrite the percent as a decimal and multiply.

$0.55 \cdot 80 = 44$          55% of 80 is 44.          A ticket costs $44.

■ Set up a proportion and solve using equivalent ratios or cross products.

$\frac{55}{100} = \frac{n}{80}$ $n = 44$.          55% of 80 is 44.          A ticket costs $44.

## Use Percents to Find Totals

To review methods for how to use percents to find totals, consider this problem:

Twelve students, or 60% of a college soccer team, are from the Midwest. How many students are on the soccer team?

■ Use a diagram to find a total value, given a percent and part.

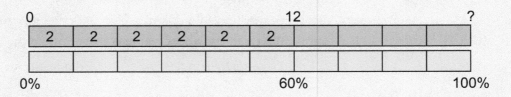

Since each 10% is equivalent to 2 students, 100% is equivalent to 20 students.

■ Write an equation and solve.

60% of $n$ is 12. Therefore, $0.6n = 12$ and $n = 20$ students.

## Determine the Percent

To review finding a percent when you know the part and the total, consider this problem:

The amount of sodium in one serving of juice is 25 mg. If the recommended amount of sodium is 3,300 mg per day, what percent of the daily sodium allowance will you have used if you drink this juice?

■ Write the part/whole relationship as a fraction and/or decimal and then as a percent.

$$\frac{25}{3,300} \qquad \frac{25}{3,300} \approx 0.0076 \qquad 0.0076 = 0.76\%$$

There is only 0.76% sodium in one glass of juice. This is less than 1% of the recommended daily amount of sodium.

# Sales, Markups and Markdowns

- When an item is "on sale" or "discounted" by a certain percent, the price is reduced. The price is less than the original amount. There are two standard methods for solving discount and sale types of problems.

  **Method 1:** Use the percent discount to find the amount saved and subtract this amount from the original price.

  **Method 2:** Determine the percent paid for the item (100% − percent discount = percent paid) and use this percent to determine the sale price.

- Percent increase and percent decrease are comparisons of the amount of change to an original value. If the price of a dozen cookies drops from $2.00 to $1.50, the percent decrease is $\frac{0.50}{2.00}$ or 25%.

- If the price of an item, such as a $20 sweater, is marked up by a set percent (for example, 40%) and then the new price is marked down by the same percent (40%), the cost of the sweater is not the original price (that is, it is not $20!).

  $20 marked up 40%        $20 \cdot 140\% = 20 \cdot 1.40 = 28$
  Note: 140% = 100% + 40%

  $28 marked down 40%      $28 \cdot 60\% = 28 \cdot 0.60 = \$16.80$
  Note: A 40% markdown is equal to paying 60% of the full cost.

---

## MATHEMATICALLY SPEAKING

Do you know what these mathematical terms mean?

▶ discount               ▶ markup                ▶ percent decrease

▶ markdown               ▶ percent               ▶ percent increase

---

## Part 1. What did you learn?

1.  Match each percent with the equivalent fraction and decimal.

| | | | | | |
|---|---|---|---|---|---|
| **a.** | 0.5% | **e.** | $\frac{1}{2}$ | **i.** | 0.5 |
| **b.** | 50% | **f.** | $\frac{3}{25}$ | **j.** | 0.012 |
| **c.** | 12% | **g.** | $\frac{3}{250}$ | **k.** | 0.005 |
| **d.** | 1.2% | **h.** | $\frac{1}{200}$ | **l.** | 0.12 |

2.  Determine whether each of the following percents is closest to 0, $\frac{1}{4}$, $\frac{1}{2}$ or 1.

    a. 0.25%      e. 0.98%

    b. 25%        f. 102%

    c. 0.1%       g. 48.2%

    d. 21.5%

3.  40% of the tables at La Famiglia restaurant were reserved at 8:00 pm. There are 60 tables in the restaurant. Show how to find the number of tables reserved at 8:00 pm at La Famiglia restaurant using each of the following strategies:

    a. Use benchmark values.

    b. Rewrite the percent as a decimal and multiply.

    c. Set up a proportion and solve using equivalent ratios or cross products.

4.  Nina figured out that she spends 9 hours of each weekday in school or doing homework. What percent of each weekday does Nina spend in school or doing homework?

5. The students at Silver Lake Middle School took a poll of students' favorite sports. They found that water volleyball was the favorite sport of 2 or 0.25% of the students surveyed. Show or explain how to find the total number of students surveyed using each of the following strategies:

   a. Make a diagram.

   b. Write an equation and solve.

6. In December, a calendar was on sale for $25. After the New Year, it was marked 40% off. What was the sale price after the New Year?

7. Glenda's Gardening store had a one-day sale. A wheelbarrow that normally sells for $125 was on sale for $100. What was the percent discount?

8. Peter builds wooden birdhouses. The materials cost $12 per birdfeeder. Peter marks up the price by 20% in order to make a profit. What is the selling price for each birdfeeder?

9. Hal's appliance store buys refrigerators from the manufacturer for $450 each and sells them for $1,575.

   a. What is the percent increase in the amount a consumer pays for this refrigerator?

   b. Hal's is having a sale and all refrigerators will be reduced by 30%. If your family buys a new refrigerator at the sale price, and the sales tax is 6% of the cost, what is the total price for a new refrigerator?

10. Gillian was asked the following question on a recent quiz.

> A T-shirt that normally sells for $40 was on sale for 30% off. What is the sale price of the T-shirt?

Here is what Gillian did to get the answer: $40 * 0.3 = 12$. So, she wrote that the T-shirt costs $12.

Gillian's answer was marked wrong. Why? What could you do or say to help Gillian find and fix her error?

11. Nikko was asked the following multiple-choice question on a recent quiz.

> 20% of the songs on Sammy's MP3 player are rock songs. Sammy has 80 rock songs on her MP3 player. How many songs are on her MP3 player in total?
>
> **A.** 20        **C.** 40
>
> **B.** 100       **D.** 400

Nikko chose letter A, but his answer was marked wrong. Draw a percent bar to help Nikko better understand the problem. Explain how to use the bar and correctly solve the problem.

Puzzling Proportions: Focusing
on Rates, Percents and Similarity

## Part 1: What did you learn?

### SECTION 1

1. In the table below, *x* represents the side length of an equilateral triangle, and *y* represents its perimeter. Copy and complete the table.

| x | y |
|---|---|
| 1 | |
| 3.5 | |
| 7 | |
| 10.25 | |
| 12 | |

2. Use the chart from Question 1 to do the following:

   a. Write a sentence, in words only, that expresses the relationship between the length of a side of an equilateral triangle and its perimeter.

   b. Write an equation that describes the relationship between the length of a side of an equilateral triangle, *x*, and its perimeter, *y*.

   c. Is the relationship between the length of a side of an equilateral triangle, *x*, and its perimeter, *y*, proportional? Why or why not?

   d. Imagine a graph of this relationship. What will it look like? What is the slope of the line?

3. Meena planted only tomatoes and peppers in her garden. The ratio of tomato plants to pepper plants in her garden is 0.75.

   a. Express this ratio using the phrase "for every."

   b. Express this ratio using the phrase "times as many."

   c. If Meena has a total of 28 plants in her garden, how many are tomato plants and how many are pepper plants? How do you know?

4. A person's walking rate is the distance they walk in a given period of time. Holly walks 2 miles in 34 minutes. Write two different rates using these values.

5. The Mega-Movie Rental Store offers movies on DVD and Blu-ray to rent. The store manager recently completed an inventory of the store and found that 80% of all the movies were on DVD.

   a. If the store owns a total of 400 movies, how many are on DVD? How many are on Bu-ray? How do you know?

   b. Describe the comparison of DVD to Blu-ray movies in the store using a part-to-part ratio expressed in simplest form.

6. Solve each proportion using the fixed value of the ratio, scaling or cross products.

   a. $\frac{3}{9} = \frac{7}{x}$

   b. $\frac{10}{5} = \frac{x}{4}$

   c. $\frac{36}{x} = \frac{12}{11}$

   d. $\frac{3}{x} = \frac{5}{10}$

   SECTION 2

7. What do each of the following scales mean?

   a. 5:1

   b. 0.25 inch to 1 foot

   c. 1:650

8. Each of the scales from Question 7 can be used to describe one of the situations below. Match each scale with the most appropriate situation.

   a. A scale model of the Empire State Building

   b. A scale drawing of a fruit fly

   c. A scale model of a house

9. The drawing below has a scale of 1:20. Using your centimeter ruler, find the indicated length of the actual duck in centimeters.

10. In the drawing below, *ABCD* ~ *EFGH*.

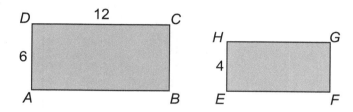

a. List the four pairs of corresponding angles.

b. Form a ratio that compares each side length on *ABCD* to its corresponding side length on *EFGH*. Are the ratios formed from each pair of corresponding sides equivalent?

c. Give the scale factor for the rectangles if *ABCD* is the original shape and it is reduced to form *EFGH*.

d. Give the scale factor if *EFGH* is the original shape and it is enlarged to form *ABCD*.

11. Copy and complete the table.

| | Dimensions | Perimeter (cm) | Area (cm²) |
|---|---|---|---|
| Original rectangle | 12 × 8 | | |
| Enlargement × 2.5 | | | |
| Reduction × 0.25 | | | |

a. Generalize. If a rectangle's dimensions change by a scale factor of *n*, what is the change in perimeter? Why?

b. Generalize. If a rectangle's dimensions change by a scale factor of *n*, what is the change in area? Why?

**12.** Copy and complete the table.

| Table of *x*- and *y*-Values | Ratio that Relates the *y*-Values to the *x*-Values | Value of the Ratio that Relates the *y*-Values to the *x*-Values | Graph | Slope of the Line |
|---|---|---|---|---|
| **a.** <table><tr><td>*x*</td><td>*y*</td></tr><tr><td>0</td><td>0</td></tr><tr><td>2</td><td>4.8</td></tr><tr><td>5</td><td></td></tr><tr><td>10</td><td>24</td></tr></table> | | | | |
| **b.** <table><tr><td>*x*</td><td>*y*</td></tr><tr><td>0</td><td>0</td></tr><tr><td>4</td><td></td></tr><tr><td></td><td>12</td></tr><tr><td>40</td><td></td></tr></table> | | 0.75 | | |
| **c.** <table><tr><td>*x*</td><td>*y*</td></tr><tr><td>0</td><td>0</td></tr><tr><td></td><td>1</td></tr><tr><td></td><td>4</td></tr><tr><td>20</td><td></td></tr></table> | | | | |

13. Given $x$- and $y$-variables that have a proportional relationship, explain how you can use the table of $x$- and $y$-values to find the ratio that relates the $y$-values to the $x$-values.

14. Jerry has been learning about proportional relationships between $x$- and $y$-variables. Explain how ratios are used to represent lines through the origin on the coordinate plane.

SECTION 3

15. There are 850 kinds of bats. Bats make up 20% of the world's mammal species. How many mammal species are there? Show your work.

16. There are 40 species of bats in North America. 70% of these species are insect eaters. How many species of bats in North America are insect eaters? Show your work.

17. Teresa earned 174 out of 300 total votes in the Student Council election. What percent of the total votes did Teresa receive? Show your work.

18. A coat that normally costs $80 is on sale for 20% off. Find the sales price of the coat using two different methods. Show your work.

19. Ned wants to buy a video game that costs $45. But he also needs to pay the sales tax of 5.25%. Ned has exactly $50 in cash. Does he have enough money for the video game? Why or why not?

20. On average, Joan paid 22% more for gas in 2008 than she paid in 2007. If $2.50 was the average cost per gallon of gas in 2007, how much did Joan pay for gas, per gallon, in 2008? Show your work.

21. Nadia and her family travel throughout the United States during the summer. Nadia figured out that she has visited 72% of the 50 states. How many states has Nadia visited? Show your work.

22. The area (in square miles) of Montana is approximately 150% of the area of Colorado. The area of Colorado, rounded to the nearest ten thousand, is 100,000 square miles. What is the area of Montana rounded to the nearest ten thousand? Show your work.

23. Merji, a middle school student, was asked the following question on a recent test:

> This year, 360 people attended the Fall Fair at Foster Middle School. This number is 120% of the attendance at last year's Fall Fair. How many people attended the fair last year?

Merji used a proportion to solve the problem:

$$\frac{x}{360} = \frac{12}{100} \qquad x = 43$$

So, about 43 people attended the fair last year.

What is wrong with Merji's reasoning? What could you say or do to help her find and fix her error?

24. Don was asked the following multiple-choice question on a recent quiz:

> Two triangles, *ABC* and *DEF*, are similar. Triangle *ABC* has 25 times the area of triangle *DEF*. What is the scale factor from triangle *ABC* to *DEF*?
>
> A. 5      C. $\frac{1}{5}$
>
> B. 25      D. $\frac{1}{25}$

Don chose letter D, but his answer was marked wrong. He asked his friend, Sam, what the right answer was. Sam said, "I don't know, I put down letter A and I got it wrong too." What is Don doing wrong? What is Sam doing wrong? What is the correct answer to this question? Why?

**congruent** Having the same size and shape.

**Example:**
Two line segments of the same length are congruent.

Two regular polygons with the same number of sides and same side lengths are congruent.

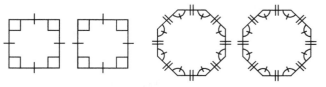

Two polygons with corresponding angles of the same measure and corresponding sides of the same length are congruent.

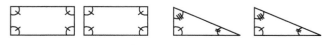

**constant** A value that does not vary.

**Example:**
In the expression $x + 3$, 3 is a constant. In the formula $A = \pi r^2$, "pi" is a constant.

**constant of proportionality** The constant (numerical value) that is equivalent to the ratio of two proportional quantities.

**Example:**
If $x$ and $y$ are proportional, $\frac{y}{x} = k$ and $y = kx$, where $k$ is the constant of proportionality.

The circumference, $C$, and the radius, $r$, of a circle are proportional. $C = 2\pi r$ and $\frac{C}{r} = 2\pi$. Therefore, the constant of proportionality is $2\pi$.

**corresponding angles** Angles that have the same relative position in two related figures.

**Example:**
$\square ABCD \sim \square EFGH$. In the similar parallelograms, $\angle A$ corresponds to $\angle E$, $\angle B$ corresponds to $\angle F$, $\angle C$ corresponds to $\angle G$ and $\angle D$ corresponds to $\angle H$.

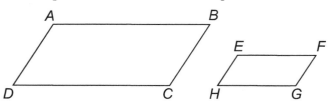

**corresponding sides**  Sides that have the same relative position in two related figures.

**Example:**

$\triangle ABC \cong \triangle DEF$. In the congruent triangles, $\overline{AB}$ corresponds to $\overline{DE}$, $\overline{BC}$ corresponds to $\overline{EF}$ and $\overline{CA}$ corresponds to $\overline{FD}$.

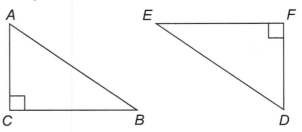

**cross products**  The results of multiplying the denominator of the first ratio in a proportion by the numerator of the second and the numerator of the first ratio by the denominator of the second. In a proportion, the cross products are equal.

**Example:**

$\frac{2}{5} = \frac{6}{15}$     $2 \cdot 15 = 5 \cdot 6 = 30$

$\frac{4.2}{10} = \frac{6.3}{15}$     $4.2 \cdot 15 = 10 \cdot 6.3 = 63$

**direct proportion**  See *direct variation*.

**direct variation**  A relationship between two quantities such that one is a constant multiple of the other. Two quantities in a direct variation are proportional.

**Example:**

If $a$ is directly proportional to $b$, the equation relating the variables is of the form $a = kb$, where $k$ is a constant.

A cashier is paid $8.50 per hour. There is a direct variation between the cashier's pay, $p$, and the number of hours worked, $h$. $p = 8.50h$.

**discount**  An amount deducted from the usual price of an item.

**Example:**

The newspaper has a $5 discount coupon for DVDs.

In January, the local department store offered a discount of 40% off all holiday items. A roll of $10.00 wrapping paper was $4.00 off.

**enlargement** A representation whose dimensions are larger than those of the original object.

**Example:**
The following objects have been enlarged from their original size.

Bone Cell

**equivalent ratios** Ratios that have the same value.

**Example:**
The following are sets of equivalent ratios:

$$\frac{5}{8} = \frac{15}{24} = \frac{22.5}{36} = \frac{55}{88} = 0.625$$

$$\frac{11}{2} = \frac{33}{6} = \frac{60.5}{11} = \frac{121}{22} = 5.5$$

**fixed value (of a proportional relationship)**
The quotient $y \div x$ when $y$ is proportional to $x$; the constant of proportionality.

**Example:**
An economy car gets 30 miles to the gallon. This is the fixed value of the ratio of the number of miles driven, $m$, and the amount of gas used, $g$.

**image** The representation of an object after an enlargement or reduction.

**Example:**

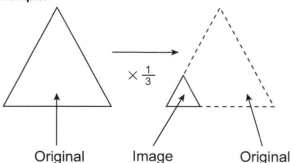

Original     Image     Original

**linear dimension** A length measure along a line segment that is part of an object or shape.

**Example:**
Three linear dimensions of a rectangle are the measures of its length, width and diagonal.

Two linear dimensions of a circle are the measures of its diameter and radius.

**markdown** A reduction in the price of an item.

**Example:**
During a sale, the sweater price indicated a markdown of 30%. The sweater was reduced from $60.00 to $42.00.

A music store was going out of business, so all CDs were marked down 75%. A $10.00 CD was reduced to $2.50.

**markup** An increase in the price of an item.

**Example:**
In order to make a profit, the clothing store owner calculated a 90% markup from his cost to determine the sale price of a pair of jeans. He buys jeans for $30.00 and sells them for $57.00.

**multiplicative comparison** A comparison of two objects using multiplication.

**Example:**
Sue is twice as tall as Megan. If $s$ is Sue's height and $m$ is Megan's height, then $s = 2m$.

The price of a CD is three-fourths that of a DVD. If a CD costs $c$ and a DVD costs $d$, then $c = \frac{3}{4}d$.

**part-to-part ratio** A ratio comparing a part or portion of a group or collection to another part or portion of a group or collection. A part-to-part ratio is often written using the colon notation $a : b$, read "*a* to *b*."

**Example:**
Of 15 balloons in a bunch, 5 were yellow, 6 were red and 4 were blue. The ratio of red balloons to yellow balloons was $6 : 5$.

At lunch, 3 friends ate sandwiches and 2 ate pasta. The ratio of sandwich eaters to pasta eaters was $3 : 2$.

**part-to-whole ratio** A ratio comparing a part or portion of a group or collection to the entire group or collection. A part-to-whole ratio is often written using the fraction notation $\frac{a}{b}$, read "*a* to *b*."

**Example:**
Of 15 balloons in a bunch, 5 were yellow, 6 were red and 4 were blue. The ratio of red balloons to all balloons was $\frac{6}{15}$ (6 to 15 or $6 : 15$).

At lunch, 3 friends ate sandwiches and 2 ate pasta. The ratio of sandwich eaters to friends was $\frac{3}{5}$ (3 to 5 or $3 : 5$).

**percent** A part-to-whole ratio that compares an amount to 100. The % symbol or the phrase "per cent" replaces the 100 in the second term of the ratio.

**Example:**
The class average on the test was $\frac{89}{100}$ or 89%.

The 50% off sale means a savings of 50¢ for every $1.00 spent.

**percent decrease** A percent representation of the ratio of the amount of change compared to an original value when the new value is less than the original.

**Example:**
After the holiday, the price of a package of decorations went from $9.99 to $4.99. This represented a decrease of $5.00 and a percent decrease of $\frac{5.00}{9.99} \approx 0.5005 = 50.05\%$.

**percent increase** A percent representation of the ratio of the amount of change compared to an original value when the new value is more than the original.

**Example:**
With a large snowfall predicted, the price of a snow shovel went from $12.50 to $19.99. This represented an increase of $7.49 and a percent increase of $\frac{7.49}{12.50} \approx 0.5992 = 59.92\%$.

**proportion** An equation stating that two ratios are equal.

**Example:**
$$\frac{a}{b} = \frac{c}{d} \text{ or } a:b = c:d$$
$$\frac{2}{7} = \frac{8}{28}$$

**proportional** A relationship between two quantities $a$ and $b$ such that for all values of $a$ and $b$ with $b \neq 0$, $\frac{a}{b} = k$, where $k$ is a constant. It follows that $a$ and $b$ are proportional if $a = k \cdot b$.

**Example:**
The perimeter, $p$, of any square is proportional to the length of its sides, $s$. For all squares, $\frac{p}{s} = 4$ and $p = 4s$.

The length of an object in feet, $f$, is proportional to its length in yards, $y$. For any measure, $\frac{f}{y} = 3$ and $f = 3y$.

**rate** A comparison or relationship between two quantities that have different units of measure.

**Example:**
The average rate of a car that traveled 60 miles in 2 hours was $\frac{60 \text{ miles}}{2 \text{ hours}} = 30$ mph.

The water in the dam fell over the spillway at a rate of $\frac{1,000 \text{ cubic feet}}{3 \text{ hours}}$.

**ratio** A comparison or relationship between two quantities $a$ and $b$, stated as "$a$ to $b$" and represented as $a : b$ or $\frac{a}{b}$.

**Example:**
The ratio representing the number of cars to the number of wheels in a parking lot is $\frac{1}{4}$ or $1:4$.

In a recipe calling for 3 cups of flour and 2 cups of sugar, the ratio of cups of flour to cups of sugar is $3:2$.

**reduction** A representation whose dimensions are smaller than the original object.

**Example:**

The following objects have been reduced from their original size.

**scale** The ratio of the size of a representation (drawing or model) of an object to the size of the actual object. This ratio compares a linear dimension of the scale drawing to the corresponding linear dimension on the original object.

**Example:**

Scale of $\frac{2}{1}$ indicates a 2:1 enlargement.

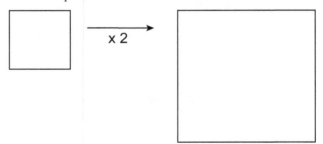

**scale drawing** A drawing that proportionally represents a real object, but is smaller or larger than the original object.

**Example:**

Large Bacteria
Scale of 15:1

Seahorse
Scale of 1:4.3

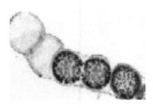  

**scale factor** A single-number value of the scale ratio used as a multiplier to either enlarge or reduce dimensions of an original object.

**Example:**

Scale factor of $\frac{1}{3}$ indicates a 1:3 reduction.

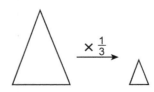

**scale model**  Three dimensional enlargements or reductions of real objects.

**Example:**

The corvette Matchbox® car was a 1 : 64 scale model.

The parade featured scale model balloons of several cartoon characters.

**similar**  Having the same shape, but not necessarily the same size. In similar figures, corresponding angles are congruent and corresponding sides are in proportion.

**Example:**

$\square ABCD \sim \square EFGH$

$\angle A \cong \angle E, \angle B \cong \angle F, \angle C \cong \angle G, \angle D \cong \angle H$

$\dfrac{AB}{EF} = \dfrac{BC}{FG} = \dfrac{CD}{GH} = \dfrac{DA}{HE}$

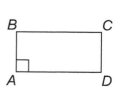

**simplest form of a ratio**  A ratio whose two quantities are whole numbers with no common factors.

**Example:**

The simplest form of 8 : 2 is 4 : 1.

The simplest form of $\dfrac{14}{91}$ is $\dfrac{2}{13}$.

**slope**  A value indicating the "steepness" of a line. The ratio of the vertical change to the horizontal change between two points on a line or line segment.

**Example:**

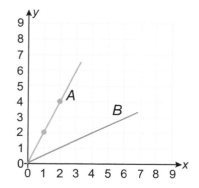

Line $A$ is steeper, and therefore has a greater positive slope, than line $B$.

Using the points (1, 2) and (2, 4), the slope of line $A$ is $\dfrac{(4-2)}{(2-1)} = \dfrac{2}{1} = 2$.

symbol "≅"  Congruent.

**Example:**
Read $\angle C \cong \angle F$ as "angle $C$ is congruent to angle $F$."

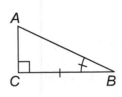
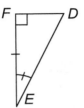

symbol "~"  Similar.

**Example:**
Read $PQR \sim STU$ as "triangle $PQR$ is similar to triangle $STU$."

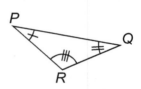
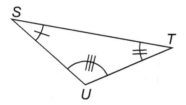

**unit rate**  A comparison of two measures where the second measure has a value of 1. A rate that, when expressed as a fraction, has a denominator of 1.

**Example:**
45 mph represents a unit rate of 45 miles per 1 hour.

Three cases of soda contain 36 cans of soda. The unit rate is 12 cans per 1 case.

**value of a ratio**  The single number representation of the ratio. It is the value of the multiplier in a multiplicative comparison.

**Example:**
Sue is twice as tall as Megan, so the value of the ratio of Sue's height to Megan's height is 2. The ratio comparing their heights is $\frac{2}{1}$ or $2:1$. If $s$ is Sue's height and $m$ is Megan's height, then $s = 2m$ and $\frac{s}{m} = 2$.

## Lesson 1.3

**On Your Own**

> **Page 22, Question 4c:** Birth rates are comparisons to 1,000, not 100.

## Lesson 2.4

**On Your Own**

> **Page 91, Question 6a:** It is not the scale factor!

> **Page 91, Question 6b:** It is not the scale factor!

# Index

## M

CPSIA information can be obtained
at www.ICGtesting.com
Printed in the USA
LVHW010317170721
692812LV00002B/2

9 780757 567049